KILLER
HEELS

KILLER HEELS

THE ART OF THE HIGH-HEELED SHOE

Edited by Lisa Small

Essays by Lisa Small, Stefano Tonchi, and Caroline Weber

New photography by Jay Zukerkorn

With contributions by Ghada Amer and Reza Farkhondeh; Gabriel Asfour, Adi Gil, and Angela Donhauser; Brian Atwood; Zach Gold; Zaha Hadid; Julian Hakes; Pierre Hardy; Steven Klein; Nick Knight; Rem D. Koolhaas; Masaya Kushino; Alessandra Lanvin; Chau Har Lee; Christian Louboutin; Julia Lundsten; Marilyn Minter; Rashaad Newsome; Cat Potter; Winde Rienstra; Elizabeth Semmelhack; and René van den Berg and Karin Janssen

Brooklyn Museum

in association with
DelMonico Books · Prestel
Munich · London · New York

CONTENTS

FOREWORD

The high-heeled shoe is the fashion world's most iconic and coveted object. *Killer Heels: The Art of the High-Heeled Shoe* offers a new perspective on this very evocative fashion item and its outsized place in the cultural imagination. Bringing together more than 160 often truly spectacular historical and contemporary high heels, and six newly commissioned and provocative short films about high heels, the exhibition explores the connection between high heels and fantasy, power, and identity.

Killer Heels follows some twenty years after *Fancy Feet: A Historic Collection of Ladies' Footwear from the Brooklyn Museum* (1993), a highly successful exhibition drawn from the Museum's extensive and renowned costume collection. In a landmark collection-sharing partnership that provided for optimal stewardship of this fragile and invaluable resource, the Museum's costume holdings were transferred to the Metropolitan Museum of Art in 2009. The newly created Brooklyn Museum Costume Collection at The Metropolitan Museum of Art was celebrated in *High Style: Masterworks from the Brooklyn Museum Costume Collection at The Metropolitan Museum of Art*, presented at the Brooklyn Museum in 2010. We are grateful to our colleagues at the Metropolitan Museum of Art for their stewardship of this rich collection, and for their partnership, which enables us to incorporate this exciting and popular material in exhibitions such as *Killer Heels*.

I also extend sincere thanks to the Bata Shoe Museum and the many other extraordinarily generous institutions and individuals who have loaned their objects to us. Special thanks are due to Stefano Tonchi, Editor-in-Chief of *W* magazine, who, along with his exceptional staff, shared our enthusiasm for this project from the beginning. His advice and the captivating essay he has contributed to this volume have helped ensure the project's success. I am also grateful to Caroline Weber, Associate Professor of French at Barnard College, for her captivating and illuminating essay, as well as to the designers and other individuals for their insightful contributions to the catalogue. The diverse artists who made the six films for the exhibition and provided statements and images for this volume—Ghada Amer and Reza Farkhondeh, Zach Gold, Steven Klein, Nick Knight, Marilyn Minter, and Rashaad Newsome—have enriched the project immeasurably. I would particularly like to thank Zach Gold, who originally approached me with the intriguing idea of incorporating fashion film—the burgeoning genre that his own work so well exemplifies—within an exhibition on high heels.

At the Brooklyn Museum, I am pleased to acknowledge once again the efforts of our exceptional staff for their work on all phases of this project. Lisa Small, Curator of Exhibitions, expertly oversaw all aspects of the exhibition and publication, developing an engaging thematic approach to these extraordinary designs, and Matthew Yokobosky, Chief Designer, created—as always—an alluring and exciting installation. The many other individuals on staff who have ensured the success of *Killer Heels* through their own significant contributions are named in the Acknowledgments that follow.

For the ongoing support of the Museum's Trustees, we extend special gratitude to Elizabeth A. Sackler, Chair, and to every member of our Board. Without the confidence and active engagement of our Trustees, it would not be possible to initiate and maintain the high level of exhibition and publication programming exemplified by *Killer Heels: The Art of the High-Heeled Shoe*.

Arnold L. Lehman
Shelby White and Leon Levy Director
Brooklyn Museum

Prada. Wedge Sandal in Rosso, Bianco, and Nero Leather, Spring/Summer 2012 (No. 165)

7

PREFACE AND ACKNOWLEDGMENTS

High heels and other elevated shoes have been status symbols for centuries. Coveted, adored, reviled, regulated, mocked, fetishized, and legislated against, they have also been central to the construction and performance of femininity.[1] In the seventeenth century, the Venetian nun and writer Arcangela Tarabotti observed that the high platform shoes called chopines (see No. 4) expressed a woman's dignity by rightfully elevating her "above the earthly triviality."[2] In contrast, a visitor to Venice during the same period, Thomas Coryate, found chopines to be the height of foolishness: "I saw a woman fall a very dangerous fall, as she was going down the staires of one of the little stony bridges with her high Chapineys alone by her selfe: but I did nothing pitty her, because she wore such frivolous and . . . ridiculous instruments, which were the occasion of her fall."[3] Loved and despised, high heels are perhaps the most polarizing item of clothing still worn daily by millions of women around the world.

The cultural meanings and messages of high heels, and the values and motives ascribed to the women who wear them, are still contested. The male CEO of a health-care start-up recently tweeted a picture of the stiletto-shod feet of a woman he saw at a technology conference, accompanied by this message and hashtag: "Event supposed to be for entrepreneurs, VCs, but these heels (I've seen several like this) . . . WTF? #brainsnotrequired." In the Twitter storm that followed, the CEO dismissed accusations of sexism, stereotyping, and upholding a double standard by equating high heels with superficiality, stupidity, and poor health choices. What the men attending the event were wearing—sneakers, hoodies?—and what those sartorial choices may have said about them, went unremarked.[4]

Another instance of the high heel as cultural flash point came when the author of a *Washington Post* article about the career and accomplishments of the White House legal counsel Kathryn Ruemmler made a point of mentioning the high heels by Christian Louboutin and Manolo Blahnik she wore to work, footwear that led some to dub her the "superstar litigatrix."[5] Her wardrobe of expensive heels was deemed so significant as to warrant its own brief sidebar article, which stated, "We tried to get a photo from the White House showing one of these exceptional pairs; instead we got this shot of her in a senior staff meeting with the president, revealing a conventional pair of heels."[6] It is hard to imagine an article about a highly accomplished man displaying the same level of interest—or insinuation—about his choice of necktie. Like the high heel, the necktie is a gendered accessory that is associated with sexual display (in this case, as a phallic object), but as an accepted accoutrement of *masculine* dress, it is perceived as an essential symbol of power.

Yet high heels were also once symbols of male power and prestige. Upper-class European men wore prominently heeled shoes by the early seventeenth century, most likely inspired by Persian riding boots (see Fig. 19). They were an integral element in the male costume of privilege and monarchy, as the writer William Makepeace Thackeray noted in his assessment of Hyacinthe Rigaud's famous portrait of King Louis XIV (see Fig. 6): "Majesty is made out of the wig, the high-heeled shoes, and cloak, all fleurs-de-lis bespangled. As for the little lean, shrivelled, paunchy old man, of five feet two. . . . Put the wig and shoes on him, and he is six feet high. . . . Thus do barbers and cobblers make the gods we worship."[7] By the mid-eighteenth century, however, men stopped wearing high heels. As an exclusively female gendered object, the high heel was considered to embody and reflect devalued attributes already culturally ascribed to women: irrationality, frivolity, vanity, and a propensity for deceitful adornment. Laden with so much historical baggage, the high heel can never be neutral. This is fully understood by all women who choose to wear them, whether they do so to express their own feelings of power and control; to radically transform their bodies, either in support of or in opposition to codes of femininity or sexual desirability; or to play with and perform conventional, transgressive, or other identities.

Killer Heels: The Art of the High-Heeled Shoe presents a selection of more than 160 contemporary and historical high heels and other elevated women's shoes, dating from approximately 1600 through the present day. Comprising shoes by well-known and emerging shoe designers and fashion houses, the exhibition includes the archetypal forms of the elevated shoe: the stiletto, the original killer heel and icon of fantasy and fetish; the wedge, a melding of height and stability; and the platform, the oldest form of elevated shoe and the one that has encompassed some of the most extreme and flamboyant designs in footwear history. The designs—some traditional and some conceptual—explore the sculptural, architectural, and artistic possibilities of the high heel, often using innovative or unexpected materials or techniques. Displaying surprising structures and shapes, many push the limits of functionality and even legibility, subverting expectations of what a high heel is or how it can look.

In addition to the shoes, the exhibition features six short films about high heels made by the artists Ghada Amer and Reza Farkhondeh, Zach Gold, Steven Klein, Nick Knight, Marilyn Minter, and Rashaad Newsome. Commissioned specifically for this exhibition, these works consider the meanings and mythologies of the high heel through a medium that has contributed so much to its iconic profile in popular culture.

This catalogue of the exhibition begins with an introductory essay by Stefano Tonchi that explores the mystique and transformative power of high heels. Caroline Weber then provides a historical overview of the various incarnations of high heels and other elevated shoes, and their complicated connections to eroticism and empowerment. The catalogue is organized into six thematic sections—Revival and Reinterpretation, Rising in the East, Glamour and Fetish, Architecture, Metamorphosis, and Space Walk—followed by the films. Many of these multivalent high-heel designs span thematic categories, allowing for endless cross-reference: there are futuristic and architectural stilettos, architectural shoes that are also metamorphic, and metamorphic shoes that are also futuristic, and so on. "Speaking of Heels" gathers together comments from several of the designers represented in the exhibition, along with Elizabeth Semmelhack, Senior Curator of the Bata Shoe Museum. These remarks, grouped by topic, have been selected from their responses to questions posed about subjects such as their inspirations, their design processes, and the cultural significance of high heels.

The narrative of eros, empowerment, and play described and illustrated in *Killer Heels* continues to evolve, as the January 27, 2014, cover of *Time* magazine suggests. The *Time* cover shows a tiny, flailing man, dressed in a business suit, hanging from the high heel of a striding, pants-clad woman. It is an image that traffics in the fetishistic trope of men being crushed under the killer heels of dangerous, domineering women. Nevertheless, the tiny man may have recognized that success may now be won by riding on the high heels—not coattails—of a powerful woman, and he is desperately trying to hang on.

Organizing this exhibition has been a pleasure and a challenge. I extend my heartfelt thanks to the many individuals whose assistance, guidance, and generosity have made it possible. First, I am very grateful to Arnold Lehman, director of the Brooklyn Museum, for his enthusiastic support of the project at every stage. I am also greatly indebted to Stefano Tonchi, Editor-in-Chief of *W* magazine, for his encouragement and advice, as well as the lively and insightful essay he contributed to this catalogue.

I would like to express my deep gratitude to the many designers who kindly shared their works with us, and to their colleagues who devoted time and attention to these loans: at A SHOE CAN BE: René van den Berg, Karin Janssen; at Aperlaï: Alessandra Lanvin, Giorgia Viola; Tamar Areshidze; at Brian Atwood: Kate Mester; Rosanne Bergsma; at Manolo Blahnik:

Amy Smith; at Richard Braqo: Holly Robinson; at Céline: Michelle Bowers; at Chanel: Ellie Hawke, Odile Premel; Andreia Chaves; at Conspiracy: Gianluca Tamburini, Daniela Scarsi; at Christian Dior: Karen Chan; at Fendi: Lauren Blunck; at FINSK: Julia Lundsten, Jess Jones; at Tom Ford: Cliff Fleiser; at Maison Jean Paul Gaultier: Thoaï Niradeth; at Givenchy: Elizabeth van Hammée, Kiko Sih; Georgina Goodman; Julian Hakes; at Pierre Hardy: Nour Seikaly; at JANTAMINIAU: Sjors Diender; at Nicholas Kirkwood: Camille Easy, Amy Osborne, Christopher Suarez; Aoi Kotsuhiroi; Masaya Kushino; Chau Har Lee; at Christian Louboutin: Alvina Patel, Cat Staffell; Kerrie Luft; at Maison Martin Margiela. Héloïse Tezzeyre, Guillemette Duzan; at Alexander McQueen: Hongyi Huang, Charlotte Arif; at Miu Miu: Erika Albies; at Charlotte Olympia: Allison Lewis; Tea Petrovic; Cat Potter; at Prada: Christian Langbein; Winde Rienstra; at Rodarte: Laura Mulleavy, Kate Mulleavy, Alexander Englert; Iris Schieferstein; Zuzana Serbak; at Shoise: Petra Högström, Matilda Maroti; at Christian Siriano: Jocelyn Warman, Bianca Bianconi; Victoria Spruce; at Sputniko!: Osaka Koichiro; at Walter Steiger: Melody Rahimi; at Noritaka Tatehana: Sophia Richfield; at threeASFOUR: Gabriel Asfour, Adi Gil, Angela Donhauser; at United Nude: Andrew Kiernan, Rem D. Koolhaas, Saskia Wesseling; at Viktor & Rolf: Katie Garrabrant Hayes; at Roger Vivier: Bruno Frisoni, Cristina Malgara, Marie Ecot, Sarah Hauser; Atalanta Weller; at Vivienne Westwood: Kiko Gaspar, Frances Knight-Jacobs; at Giuseppe Zanotti: Alessandra Peruzzo-Alter, Emmanuel Tomasini.

Several other institutions and individuals also facilitated key loans: Stefania Ricci, Martina Santoro, and Paola Gusella at the Museo Ferragamo; Eva Frosch at Frosch Portmann; Kate Scheyer and Marie-Amélie Sauvé; and Thierry-Maxime Loriot, Diane Charbonneau, and Anne-Marie Chevrier at the Montreal Museum of Fine Arts. I owe a great debt to Giovanna Campagna, Sarah Kalagvano, and Caroline Wolff at *W* magazine, who patiently and kindly helped me sort out many crucial logistical details.

This exhibition includes stellar examples of historical high-heeled footwear drawn from the Costume Institute at the Metropolitan Museum of Art, including objects from the Brooklyn Museum Costume Collection at The Metropolitan Museum of Art. I am extraordinarily grateful to Harold Koda, Elizabeth Bryan, Sarah Scaturro, Bethany Matia, and Amanda Garfinkel for their help making these loans and crucial photography possible. I also want to extend my profound thanks to Elizabeth Semmelhack, not only for generously lending us significant historical footwear from the Beta Shoe Museum, further enriching our presentation, but for being a gracious and inspirational colleague; her critical scholarship and insights about the history and cultural significance of high heels have been invaluable to me in the preparation of this exhibition and catalogue.

I am also exceptionally grateful to the seven artists—Ghada Amer and Reza Farkhondeh, Zach Gold, Steven Klein, Nick Knight, Marilyn Minter, and Rashaad Newsome—who made original short films for *Killer Heels*.

Caroline Weber's engaging and informative essay on the history of high heels adds immeasurably to the scope of this publication. I am also indebted to the designers—Gabriel Asfour, Adi Gil, and Angela Donhauser; Brian Atwood; Zaha Hadid; Julian Hakes; Pierre Hardy; Rem D. Koolhaas; Masaya Kushino; Alessandra Lanvin; Chau Har Lee; Christian Louboutin; Julia Lundsten; Cat Potter; Winde Rienstra; Elizabeth Semmelhack; and René van den Berg and Karin Janssen—who not only loaned their works to the exhibition but also shared thoughtful and illuminating responses for the "Speaking of Heels" section of the book.

I am grateful to the many staff members at the Brooklyn Museum who contributed their expertise and unflagging energy to ensure the success of this exhibition and catalogue. Kevin Stayton, Chief Curator, offered his encouragement as well as his great knowledge of the Brooklyn Museum's costume collection. My current and former colleagues in the Exhibitions Division—Sharon Matt Atkins, Dolores Farrell, Emily Annis, Lisa Genna, Sara Devine, Holly Harmon, Amanda Dietz, Tricia Laughlin Bloom, and interns Constance Clarisse and Coby Lerner—were a source of great moral and organizational support in every phase of this project. I am especially obliged to Katie Welty, project registrar, who expertly orchestrated the many complicated loans, with the support of Liz Reynolds, Chief Registrar, and the help of Naomi Brown. Ken Moser, Vice Director for Collections, has overseen all logistics. I am thankful to Lisa Bruno, conservator, along with Michael Mandina, mount maker, for making these objects look their best. Walter Andersons, Collections Manager, and members of his staff provided essential assistance in the photo shoot and the installation. Deirdre Lawrence and the staff of the Art Reference Library were a great help with research. I also want to acknowledge Richard Aste, Curator of European Art; Susan Beningson, Assistant Curator of Asian Art; Teresa A. Carbone, Andrew W. Mellon Curator of American Art; Joan Cummins, Lisa and Bernard Selz Curator of Asian Art; Barry R. Harwood, Curator of Decorative Arts; and Eugenie Tsai, John and Barbara Vogelstein Curator of Contemporary Art, for allowing me to enhance the exhibition and catalogue with exceptional works and images from their collections, and Catherine Morris, Sackler Family Curator for the Elizabeth A. Sackler Center for Feminist Art, for her careful review of the text. I am particularly indebted to Chief Designer Matthew Yokobosky, who envisioned and executed a gorgeous exhibition design and graciously shared his boundless knowledge of fashion and film.

For guiding the progress of this volume, I am grateful to James Leggio, Head of Publications and Editorial Services, and Sallie Stutz, Vice Director of Merchandising. Joanna Ekman skillfully edited the manuscript, vastly improving it; I am profoundly thankful for her astute suggestions, meticulous attention to detail, and infinite patience. I extend my appreciation to Deborah Wythe for coordinating the photo shoot and to her staff in the Digital Lab, including Sarah DeSantis, Photographer, and Alice Cork, Picture Researcher, for their invaluable help in gathering images.

At DelMonico Books · Prestel, Mary DelMonico provided enthusiastic support for this publication, and Karen Farquhar oversaw production of the volume. Jay Zukerkorn and his assistant Andres Guillard contributed the amazing new photography that graces its pages, and Abbott Miller, with Yoon-Young Chai, at Pentagram created the stunning design.

Lisa Small

THIS IS NOT A SHOE

STEFANO TONCHI

With their increasingly vertiginous heights, crazy combinations of materials, and unimaginable shapes, these shoes are *not* made for walking—just as that pink gold watch encrusted in diamonds is *not* made to tell time, and that see-through chiffon dress is *not* made to cover the body and keep it warm. Today, more than ever in our history, such beautiful objects define who we are and underscore the performative aspect of identity. Fashion has forever divorced them from their original function and meanings.

Shoes, like all fashion, tell our stories—stories we make up for ourselves or stories we want to tell others. They are the words and punctuation that we use to communicate with each other and to create the narratives of our lives. The great shoe designer Roger Vivier aptly dubbed one of his most famous creations—a very curvaceous, slim heel (see No. 94)—"The Virgule" ("The Comma"). Other shoes are a suggestive verb or an imaginative adjective. Some shoes are a plain full stop.

Still, we might ask, why do only women wear high heels today? And why have their high heels grown out of proportion, reaching unprecedented elevation and extraordinary complexity, taking over entire conversations? For centuries, shoes have been objects of social interest, as in the elevated chopines of sixteenth-century Venice (see Nos. 4, 35). High shoes were later adapted in the European royal courts as a means for both male and female nobility to express power and exclusivity (see Fig. 6). In the nineteenth century, however, heels became the shoes that every woman needed in her wardrobe to symbolize femininity and display sex appeal.

My friend the writer Virginie Mouzat (who never takes off her high heels) says that a woman's relationship with shoes is a long history of "consensual martyrdom." It is indeed a relationship based on constraint and pain, endured in order to make the foot look smaller and to accentuate the elegant and sensual curve of its arch. This curve's powerful allure can only be compared with that of the contour of the lips and the line of the breast. Effecting a

Freudian displacement of libido, the high heel has also functioned as a prime Freudian fetish object.

In his book *High Heels: Fashion, Femininity, Seduction*, Ivan Vartanian compares heels to prostheses, artificial extensions of the legs that, like every fetishistic object, give special power to the person wearing them. This power is not only sexual. High heels change the physical posture of a woman, moving her barycenter forward, pushing the breast and the derriere out, and making her walk more erectly. She becomes precarious and imperious at the same time. But high heels also change human psychology, transforming our way of thinking about women and the way that women think about themselves. She who wears them puts herself on a pedestal, making herself more visible and more desirable, more fragile and unbalanced but also more strong and dominant. She who wears heels—especially very high heels—commands respect because she has the courage to defy gravity and walk on air.

Today, technology and design have taken shoes to never-before-seen elevations. The imaginative Japanese designer Noritaka Tatehana has created futuristic heelless elevated shoes (see No. 55). Simple stiletto heels have given way to architectonic, ever-higher heels, covered with embellishments and encrusted with extravagant decorations. They are like modern skyscrapers gone baroque and postmodern.

As unnatural and transgressive signifiers of female power and sexuality, high heels have been a perfect fit for fashion photographers, finding a special place in S and M imagery. Photographic masters such as Guy Bourdin and Helmut Newton made the relationship between heels and sexual power one of their signatures, and today's generation of great fashion photographers (Fig. 1), designers, and filmmakers, whose work is stunningly represented in this exhibition, follows their lead.

FIG. 1
The Girly Show, from *W* magazine (March 2012). Photo: Mert Alas and Marcus Piggott

(opposite) Roger Vivier. "Rendez Vous, Limited Edition Blue Feather Choc," Fall/Winter 2013–14 (No. 39)

THE ETERNAL HIGH HEEL: EROTICISM AND EMPOWERMENT

CAROLINE WEBER

At an October 2013 event in New York City honoring Tamara Mellon, the cofounder of Jimmy Choo, an unlikely speaker stepped up to the podium: Mayor Michael Bloomberg. "I like women, and I think that they look stunning in high heels," the mayor enthused to general applause, and then added, "If I were a woman, I think I would wear high heels." Improbably but intuitively, Bloomberg underscored the two key elements of the high-heeled shoe's mystique: eroticism and empowerment. To praise women's appearance in high heels was of course to invoke the sex appeal of the shoes, while to declare that he himself—a billionaire who aggressively expanded the prerogatives (and term limits) of his elected office—could envisage wearing them was to claim them for the cause of Power. It seems fitting that as preparations were under way last fall for the Brooklyn Museum's exhibition *Killer Heels*, the mayor of New York should have stressed the two themes that predominate—separately or in tandem—over the course of the high heel's long history.

In the West that history began more than two millennia ago, not with high heels as such, but rather with shoes featuring a built-up, elevated sole beneath the entire length of the foot, including the heel, arch, and ball. The earliest such style, known to the ancient Greeks as a *kothornos* and to their Roman emulators as a *cothurnus*, was a lace-up buskin with exaggeratedly thick cork soles (Fig. 2). Used by classical actors for greater visibility while performing in the round, the *cothurnus* enhanced the wearer's stature both literally and figuratively. Insofar as Greco-Roman drama tended to portray chiefly gods, goddesses, kings, and queens, it behooved the men cast as such characters to look forbidding—to loom large in the public imagination as well as in the public eye. As a result, they were outfitted with taller *cothurni* than their less important costars, such as the wizened slave women or the sagacious graybeards who made up the drama's obligatory chorus.[1] From its very inception, the elevated shoe was a theatrical

prop par excellence, designed to emphasize the wearer's distinction, both physically and symbolically.

The elevated shoe gained prominence in sixteenth-century Venice, where it was again pressed into service as a signifier of personal grandeur. Profitably poised at the crossroads of the busy oceanic trade routes linking Europe, the Americas, and Asia, Venice saw an unprecedented influx of wealth during this period, and one of the favorite status symbols of its newly rich inhabitants was a flamboyant, teetering mule called a chopine. This new, exclusively feminine variation on the platform shoe—which consisted of decoratively embroidered cloth or leather uppers attached to wooden or cork pedestals ranging from six to twenty inches in height (see No. 4)—had an ostensibly utilitarian purpose: keeping women's delicate feet dry in the soupy streets of lagoon-based Venice. Chopines were said to have been inspired by the traditional wood stilt-clogs, or *qabâqib*, that women in the Ottoman Empire, one of the Venetians' major Eastern trading partners, donned to navigate the slick tiled floors of the bathhouse, or *hammam* (Fig. 3). The Ottoman model featured two pedestals— one beneath the heel of the foot and another beneath the ball—whereas certain chopines comprised only a single pedestal, positioned under the arch at the center of the shoe. Whether equipped with one pedestal or two, chopines made walking so difficult that only ladies of considerable leisure could wear them. Usually members of Venice's plutocratic ruling class, these early fashion victims took their mincing steps supported by maids or pages conscripted to prevent them from toppling over. The ladies' showy height and incapacitation were the chopine's true raison d'être, for as beautifully ornamented

Chanel. Detail of Heel, Haute Couture, Spring/Summer 2010 (No. 27)

as the shoe often was, and as sumptuous as the materials from which it was made, the floor-length hemlines of Renaissance skirts obscured it from view. Its extravagance was visible only in the wearer's exaggerated height—as one foreign visitor noted, Venice's fairer sex appeared to be "half flesh, half wood"[2]—and its attendant, costly inconveniences (those servants, carriages, and gondolas). The taller the woman, the more flagrantly impractical was her footwear—and the more exalted, by implication, her socioeconomic standing.[3] This elite status gained further emphasis from the additional cloth—likewise a luxury good, signaling enviable wealth—that the woman's dress had to contain in order to preserve the requisite coverage of her ankles and feet.[4]

The chopine remained a prized accoutrement of feminine privilege well into the seventeenth century, mostly in Italy and Spain, though by 1600 it was already sufficiently well known in Northern Europe that Shakespeare had Prince Hamlet pronounce a female visitor to the Danish court "nearer to heaven . . . by the altitude of a chopine."[5] The style's reach may have extended all the way to China, where the Manchurian caste that came to power in the mid-seventeenth century introduced a "horse-hoof-soled," single-pedestal slipper for patrician women (see Nos. 38, 45) as an alternative to the native Chinese custom of female foot-binding.[6] The hesitant, mincing gait that the "Manchu chopine" required of its wearer, along with the trompe l'oeil effect by which its clunky, oversized sole dwarfed even an unbound foot, was held by its partisans to achieve much the same dainty, alluring femininity that ancient foot-binding practices produced, but with none of the deformation and pain.[7] A hundred years later, a dual-pedestal, thong-sandal version of this style emerged among Japan's nascent geisha culture in the form of the geta (see Nos. 33, 47); like its Manchu counterpart, the geta was thought to enhance a woman's fragile, delicate grace—the sine qua non of the geisha's rarefied erotic allure.

In its native Europe as well, the chopine came to represent sexiness as much as, or perhaps even more than, social prestige. Over time, the competitive one-upmanship among the moneyed fans of the style led to ever more exaggerated platforms, which prompted church authorities to condemn chopines as "depraved" and "dissolute."[8] These fulminations supported a widespread perception that chopines, in their flagrant excess, were courtesans' footwear of choice.[9] The shoes' putative origins in the steamy, exotic Turkish bathhouse may also have contributed to this perception, as may the ease with which they, like all mules, could be slipped off in a moment of reckless abandon. Whatever its logic, the association that took root in the public imagination between chopines and women of ill repute found its way into Renaissance visual culture. Popular images portraying chopine-shod "public women" helped forge an indelible connection between elevated feminine footwear and licentious female sexuality (Fig. 4).

In the 1590s new technical developments allowed for the construction of a high, stacked-leather heel toward the back of the shoe; a supportive, molded leather arch in the middle; and a flat sole at the front. By the mid-seventeenth century, the resulting shoe shape—the first high heel proper—edged out the chopine in upper-class women's wardrobes. It also gained widespread acceptance among upper-class men, who appreciated not only the boost in stature that the new shoe provided but also the convenient way it steadied their feet in the stirrups while riding. (Indeed, the shoe might have been inspired by the Persian riding boot, whose heel was expressly designed to stabilize the mounted cavalryman's feet in battle.)[10] For the next two

hundred years, men's footgear would differ markedly little from women's. But for both sexes, it designated high social standing, particularly in ancien régime France, where the distinctive *talon rouge* (red heel) identified the wearer as a denizen of the royal court (Fig. 5). Legend traces this look to an episode during Louis XIV's reign (1643–1715), when a group of rambunctious noblemen returned to Versailles from a wild night in Paris with the high heels of their silk shoes stained red from the bloody streets around the slaughterhouses of Les Halles. The Sun King himself lost no time in adopting the *talon rouge*, and he established it as an indispensable feature of male courtiers' dress (Fig. 6). Over the course of the eighteenth century, it was adopted by men of high rank throughout Europe, though it remained most closely associated with the grandees of Versailles, as evidenced by the first and last official portraits painted of Louis XV (r. 1715–74) and Louis XVI (r. 1774–92), respectively.[11]

After the overthrow of the French monarchy in 1792, the militant, newly enfranchised advocates of *égalité* frowned upon the elitist overtones of the *talon rouge*, and it fell from favor.[12] Ascending to power in the Revolution's aftermath, Napoleon Bonaparte (r. 1804–15) duly rejected the high *talon*, red and otherwise, as a political statement. Even the exquisite shoes he commissioned for his coronation as emperor in 1804 were completely flat,[13] as were the delicate silk slippers favored by his wife, Josephine (Fig. 7), an influential trendsetter in France and abroad. In this manner, the prerevolutionary equivalency between high shoes and high status was, in both men's and women's Western fashion, negated and reversed, and for men, at least, elevated footwear essentially disappeared for good from mainstream power dressing in the West.

For women, the high-heeled shoe returned to vogue in the final decades of the nineteenth century, once again becoming a staple of elegant dress. At the same time, its efficacy in showcasing women's secondary sexual characteristics—rearranging the wearer's spinal column in a sinuous S curve that pushed her breasts forward and her rump upward and back—appealed to the showgirls, artists' models, and *grandes horizontales* who proliferated during the Belle Époque. Unlike their "respectable" counterparts' modest, floor-skimming dresses, the scanty attire of these so-called professional beauties gave the public an unobstructed view of their heels, among other things. Édouard Manet's portrait of a Parisian courtesan, *Nana* (Fig. 8), offered a case in point. So did Henri de Toulouse-Lautrec's depictions of the brazen, high-kicking dancers of the Moulin Rouge, as well as the soft-porn "French postcard" industry, which exploited the erotic potential of photography as a medium and of high heels as a feminine attribute (Fig. 9).[14] Like Renaissance art's evocative pairing of prostitutes with chopines, fin-de-siècle visual culture reestablished a firm perceptual connection between heels and sex.

In the 1920s the flappers further emphasized this association with their flashy metallic leather, ankle-strap heels (see No. 19), which their daring, raised hemlines tantalizingly revealed.[15] Sigmund Freud also made the case for the sexual potential of women's footwear in his pioneering 1927 essay on fetishism, an impulse he ascribed to the traumatic experience of a young (male) child looking up his mother's skirt and seeing her "castrated" genitals.[16] According to Freud, the little boy found this discovery profoundly upsetting—"for if a woman had been castrated, then his own possession of a penis was in danger"— and reacted by unconsciously replacing the mother's missing penis in his mind with a proximate object, most often "her foot or shoe";[17] forever afterward, that object would hold unparalleled erotic appeal for the fetishist.

FIG. 8
Édouard Manet (French,
1832–1883). *Nana*, 1877.
Oil on canvas, 60⅝ × 45¼ in.
(154 × 115 cm). Hamburger
Kunsthalle, Hamburg,
Germany, Inv. 2376.
Bildarchiv Preussischer
Kulturbesitz, Berlin/Art
Resource, NY. Photo:
Elke Walford

FIG. 9
Jean Agélou (French,
1877–1921). Postcard,
Série 90, circa 1900–1921

FIG. 10
René Magritte (Belgian,
1898–1967). *La Philosophie
dans le Boudoir*, 1947. Oil
on canvas, 76¾ × 59⅞ in.
(195 × 152 cm). Private
collection, New York.
© 2014 C. Herscovici/Artists
Rights Society (ARS),
New York. Photo: Sotheby's,
New York. Photo courtesy
The Menil Archives, the
Menil Collection, Houston

FIG. 11
André Caillet Fils. *Gala
Wearing the Shoe-Hat
Created by Elsa Schiaparelli
from a Salvador Dalí
Design*, 1938. Gelatin silver
photograph, 9 × 11¼ in.
(23 × 28.6 cm). Fundació
Gala-Salvador Dalí, Figueres.
© 2014 Salvador Dalí,
Fundació Gala-Salvador
Dalí, Artists Rights Society
(ARS), New York

FIG. 12
Christian Dior (French,
1905–1957). Roger Vivier
(French, 1913–1998) for
House of Dior (French,
founded 1947). Pumps,
1955. Silk, metal, plastic.
The Metropolitan Museum
of Art, New York, Gift of
Valerian Stux-Rybar,
1979 (1979.472.22a, b).
Image copyright © The
Metropolitan Museum
of Art. Image source:
Art Resource, NY

Controversial as they were (and remain), Freud's theories gained heightened contemporary currency from the Paris-based Surrealist artists, whose avant-garde work linked the high-heeled shoe with a specifically fetishized female body. René Magritte's *La Philosophie dans le Boudoir* (Fig. 10), for instance, explicitly invests inanimate women's accessories (high heels and a frilly undergarment taken straight out of a French postcard) with titillating corporeality (toes and breasts). Salvador Dalí collaborated with the iconoclastic fashion designer Elsa Schiaparelli on the surrealistic but wearable "shoe hat" of 1937–38 (Fig. 11, see No. 118). With the amplified phallic shape of its inverted, upwardly jutting heel, the shoe hat effected a textbook case of fetishism, and of another phenomenon Freud called "displacement upwards," which distanced the erotic object from its genital origins and provocatively relocated it to the body's ostensible seat of rationality and self-mastery: the head.

In the wake of these developments came a slew of additional advances. In 1937 Salvatore Ferragamo revived the chopine's towering cork sole, and so brought the platform shoe into the modern era. Because of its early adoption by Hollywood film stars (Ferragamo reportedly made his 1938 "Rainbow" platform for Judy Garland; see No. 10),[18] this high style again suggested frank feminine seductiveness. Both the platform and another Ferragamo invention, the pragmatic wedge heel, soon spurred a backlash from men who, the *New York Times* reported in 1940, missed the sex appeal of "those delicate high insteps pattering along on spindle heels."[19]

Such spindle-heeled styles, not coincidentally, figured prominently in the pinup imagery of the 1930s and 1940s, but it was only after World War II, when footwear manufacturers succeeded in inserting a stabilizing steel rod into the heel of the shoe, that these confections could actually get produced.

The resulting stiletto, named for its spiky shape, promptly became synonymous with 1950s femininity. Its demure side was epitomized by Roger Vivier's pumps for Christian Dior, fitting complements to that couturier's womanly, hourglass designs (Fig. 12), and its man-killer aspect exemplified by Marilyn Monroe's sleek, custom Ferragamos. So bewitching, in fact, was Marilyn's high-heeled, hip-swinging gait—emphatically highlighted in the 116-foot walk her character took toward Niagara Falls in the 1953 film *Niagara*—that it sparked feverish speculation about how she achieved it. According to one of the most enduring accounts, proffered by the Hollywood gossip columnist Jimmy Starr, she imperceptibly shaved down one of the heels in every pair she wore; this slight unevenness, Starr theorized, produced both the little-girl precariousness and the lasciviously swaying pelvis that together defined Marilyn's extraordinary walk.[20]

The counterculture of the 1960s spurred a host of experimental heels, from Beth Levine's Eastern-inspired creations (see No. 53), whose cantilevered forms directly referenced Manchu and geisha culture, to the exuberant, gender-bending platform shoes of rock stars such as Jimi Hendrix. Updating the latter trend in the 1970s, David Bowie incorporated the platform shoe into his hyperstylized, androgynous stage costumes (Fig. 13) and so enshrined it as the ultimate glam-rock accessory. Once again, the elevated shoe sent a daring message about sexuality—in Bowie's case, his avowed bisexuality—and thereby

FIG. 13
Untitled [David Bowie], 1973.
Photo: Masayoshi Sukita.
© Masayoshi Sukita

FIG. 14 (far right, top)
Pour It Up Party, November 1,
2013. Photo: Damien Piron.
© Damien Piron

FIG. 15 (far right, bottom)
Daphne Guinness for
German *Vogue,* August
2011. Photo: Bryan Adams
Photography. © Bryan
Adams, 2011

assumed prime importance in the construction of identity. It retained its connotations of sex and power in the 1980s, but as a status symbol for the women of New York's "Nouvelle Society," wives of Wall Street's superrich whose preferences ran toward the timeless, ladylike styles of the luxury shoe designer Manolo Blahnik. (Blahnik returned the favor by naming some of his models after his best customers: the sling-back "Carolyne," still in production today, was named for Carolyne Roehm, then the wife of the takeover titan Henry Kravis.)

Nowadays, unprecedented technological innovation and creative ferment in the shoe industry are yielding wildly inventive results. Generally, locomotion in these high heels is so perilous as to necessitate the twenty-first-century equivalents of gondolas and ladies' maids: chauffeured cars and personal assistants. These accoutrements broadcast the wearer's wealth and status just as loudly as chopines or *talons rouges* ever did, and thus have found particular favor among those media-grabbing musicians, actresses, socialites, and reality stars whose ethos of unchecked conspicuous consumption and relentless personal "branding" has come to define contemporary style. For better or for worse, the singer Rihanna's latest shoe-related stunt at a nightclub—sipping a drink from what appears, on the basis of its hallmark red sole, to be a Christian Louboutin stiletto—exemplifies this impulse (Fig. 14).

Nevertheless, the most thoughtful of today's extreme-footwear devotees reveal a sophisticated sense of the high heel's history. In August 2011 the fashion maven and muse Daphne Guinness posed as David Bowie's platform-loving, she-male persona, Ziggy Stardust, for German *Vogue*

(Fig. 15). Replacing the original Stardust's chunky red sandals with glittery, spectacularly high Natacha Marro heelless platforms, Guinness both acknowledged a tradition and made it unmistakably hers. The twenty-first-century high heels presented in this exhibition— from Céline's Magritte-worthy "foot" shoes to Winde Rienstra's bondage-friendly proto-geta to FINSK's futuristic, color-blocked chopines (see Nos. 120, 50, 169)—perform the same, exquisitely elevating function, simultaneously referencing the power footwear of the past and setting it on a bold course toward the future.

REVIVAL AND REINTERPRETATION

Oscar Wilde humorously expressed the ephemeral nature of fashion when he proclaimed that it was "a form of ugliness so intolerable that we have to alter it every six months."[1] Change is the essence of fashion, but as Wilde suggests, it does not follow a strictly linear trajectory of unique moments; instead it consists of cyclical returns to earlier styles that may be reinterpreted or differentiated to some degree but remain recognizable in their former lineaments. Salvatore Ferragamo's purple wedge shoe is strikingly modern, yet it nonetheless pays homage to Italian Renaissance colors and shoe forms (see No. 3).[2] His black lace-up bootie updates the prevailing women's dress boot styles of the late nineteenth and early twentieth centuries with a higher heel and an open weave (see No. 26). Old becomes new becomes old becomes new.

Elegant eighteenth-century shoes like the delicate pink mule flying through the air in Jean-Honoré Fragonard's painting *The Swing* (Fig. 16)—made from brocaded silks, wools, and velvets, often heavily embroidered or embellished with buckles, and sporting a pointed toe and curved heel (see No. 25)—have been an enduring reference for designers like Bernard Figueroa, Manolo Blahnik, and Pietro Yantorny (see Nos. 2, 7, 25). T-strap, or bar, heels first came into fashion in the 1920s, when flappers wanted a shoe that could be shown off under rising hemlines but would not fall off as they danced the night away (Fig. 17). It continued to be a popular choice for elegant evening shoes in the 1930s (see No. 9). In 2013 Miu Miu revisited the style, adding a higher heel, a peep toe, inflated volumes, and a bright color for a Pop, cartoonlike effect (see No. 22).

Historical references and motifs can also provide a gloss to an otherwise modern style. Chanel's sleek silver bootie with pearls and a sinuous plantlike heel and Miu Miu's patent Mary Jane with a gilded foliate platform wedge both call to mind the mirrored and ornately carved interiors of the palace of Versailles (see Nos. 27, 20). (A giant sculpture of high heels made from pots and pans was recently installed there by contemporary artist Joana Vasconcelos [Fig. 18].[3]) The palace's most glamorous occupant can be recognized on the ankle strap of Christian Louboutin's playful "Marie-Antoinette" stiletto, wearing a towering pouf topped with a miniature French frigate (see No. 17).[4]

The earliest form of elevated shoe— the platform—is perhaps the style that has reappeared most often at the heights of fashion since its modern Western

1. Manolo Blahnik. "Borli,"
Spring/Summer 2014

FIG. 16 (AND DETAIL)
Jean-Honoré Fragonard
(French, 1732–1806). *The
Swing*, 1767. Oil on canvas,
31⅞ × 25½ in. (81 × 64.8 cm).
The Wallace Collection,
London. © By kind
permission of the Trustees
of the Wallace Collection

FIG. 17
Chanel. *Sketch 038-031*,
Fall 1920. Henri Bendel
Fashion and Costume
Sketch Collection.
Brooklyn Museum Libraries.
Special Collections

FIG. 18
Joana Vasconcelos
(Portuguese, born France,
1971). *Marilyn (AP)*, 2011.
Stainless steel pans and
lids, concrete, each
117 × 61 × 161½ in. (297 ×
155 × 410 cm). Collection
of the artist. Installed at
the Galerie des Glaces,
Château de Versailles,
June 16–September
30, 2012. Work produced
with the support of
Silampos, S.A. Photo: Luis
Vasconcelos/Courtesy
Unidade Infinita Projectos/
Château de Versailles

prominence by the fifteenth century. The platform chopines of Renaissance Venice connoted luxury and leisure (see Nos. 4, 35), and when designers and manufacturers, including Ferragamo and Herman Delman, first reintroduced the platform style in the 1930s as beach wear, the shoe was once again associated with leisure culture. During the 1940s platforms made with materials such as fabric, cork, wood, or raffia were considered sensible shoes. The form was sometimes styled as high-fashion evening wear, as well—mostly to the chagrin of men in the 1930s and 1940s, who did not find the chunky platform or wedge as alluring as the high heel (see Nos. 10, 29).[5]

The stiletto vanquished the platform during the post–World War II period, but platforms returned with a vengeance in the 1970s, with chunky profiles and graphic patterns that made a statement on the street and the dance floor (see Nos. 11, 13). During the era of women's liberation, the solid platform (in contrast to the spindly stiletto) provided the extra empowering inches needed to meet most men on an equal eye level. The decade also saw a revival of men's elevated shoes, a form that had been absent from fashion since the mid-eighteenth century and has not appeared since in the mainstream. Some men wore outrageous platforms, aggressively asserting their masculinity in emulation of glam rockers

and the influential "Super Fly" style showcased in the 1972 Blaxploitation film of the same name.[6]

After another retreat from fashion, platforms returned yet again in the 1990s. Designs were more streamlined, as exemplified by Vivienne Westwood's elevated court shoe, in which the platform, rather than being boldly demarcated, is concealed by the upper and paired with a thinner, towering heel (see No. 30). Designers such as Christian Louboutin have taken this style one step further to create hybrids like the "Printz" Mary Jane, which combines a concealed 3-inch platform with a staggering 7-inch stiletto heel (see No. 84).

2. Bernard Figueroa. Mule, circa 1994

3. Salvatore Ferragamo (Italian, 1898–1960). Shoe, 1948–50
4 (opposite). Italian. Chopines, 1550–1650

5. J. Ferry, Paris. Evening Slippers, 1885–90
6. Samo (Italian). Pump, circa 1968
7. Manolo Blahnik. Evening Shoe, 1990–92
8 (opposite). Roger Vivier. "Rose N' Roll," Fall 2012

9 (opposite). Delman (American). Evening Shoe, 1935–40
10 (this page). Salvatore Ferragamo (Italian, 1898–1960). Platform Sandal, 1938

11. Casuccio e Scalera per Loris Azzaro (Italian). Sandal, 1974–79
12 (opposite). Brian Atwood. "Paulina," Spring/Summer 2013

13. Mary Poppins (Italian). Platform Shoe, circa 1973
14 (opposite). Maison Martin Margiela. Boot, Artisanal Autumn/Winter 2013

15 (opposite). Pierre Hardy. Platform, Spring 2013
16 (this page). Christian Louboutin. "Clovis," Spring/Summer 1996

17 (opposite and this page, top). Christian Louboutin. "Marie-Antoinette," Fall/Winter 2008–9
18 (this page, bottom). French. Shoes, 1690–1700

19. André Perugia (French, 1893–1977). Evening Sandals, 1928–29
20 (opposite). Miu Miu. "Cammeo Baroque" Leather Wedge, Fall/Winter 2006

21. Charles Strohbeck, Inc. (American). Evening Shoe, circa 1920
22 (opposite). Miu Miu. "Ortensia and Oro" T-strap Pump, Fall/Winter 2013

23. Enzo Albanese (Italian). Shoe, 1954–58
24 (opposite, top). Italian. Shoe, 1700–1730*
25 (opposite, bottom). Pietro Yantorny (Italian, 1874–1936). Pump, 1925–30

26. Salvatore Ferragamo (Italian, 1898–1960). "Booty" Cocktail Boot, 1947
27 (opposite). Chanel. Heel, Haute Couture, Spring/Summer 2010

28 (top). John Fluevog. "Munster" Platform Shoe, 1994
29 (bottom). Delman (American), Bergdorf Goodman (American). Pump, 1937–39
30 (opposite, top). Vivienne Westwood. "Portrait" Shoe, 1990
31 (opposite, bottom). Charles Strohbeck, Inc. (American). Oxford, 1900–1910

RISING
IN THE EAST

The origins of the platforms and high heels that have dominated Western women's fashion footwear for centuries lie in the East.[1] Elevated footwear can be seen in ancient Greek statues of Aphrodite and other idealized female figures, but the style is actually evidence of the Greek fascination for things Eastern, or "Oriental." In fact, the Greeks associated the "Orient"—primarily, their adversary Persia—with foreign luxury and excess, particularly in relation to women's fashions (including elevated footwear), which were decried in many ancient treatises as dangerous and deceitful. Another Persian style, the heeled shoe worn by cavalrymen to help keep their feet in the stirrups, entered the Western fashion canon in the late sixteenth century on the feet of aristocratic men (Fig. 19). At a time of burgeoning military and trade alliances with Persia against the Ottoman Empire, European men embraced the Persian heeled shoe and its masculine aura of military prowess and adventure.

Other types of elevated footwear followed a circular pattern of influence with respect to East and West. The wood stilt-clogs called *nalin*, or *qabâqib*, worn by women in bathhouses of the Ottoman Empire to keep their feet high and dry above the wet floors, most likely descended from Roman bath shoes called *sculponea*. Because of their association with the pampered world of the harem, *nalin* became a potent symbol of feminine luxury in the West, particularly in

Venice, a city with historically close connections to the Islamic world. The elevated form of the Near Eastern *nalin*, in turn, may have influenced chopines, the high platforms that both noblewomen and courtesans of Renaissance Venice wore under their long gowns. Although their purpose has been frequently described as protective—elevating a woman's feet and garments above the filthy streets—recent scholarship suggests that chopines were in fact primarily an intimate foundational accessory, worn under skirts to create a taller, more elongated figure (Fig. 20A, B). They remained largely invisible when worn, yet were integral to their wearer's conspicuous display of wealth: their height meant that already costly dresses required extra fabric to reach the ground.

Dramatically elevated footwear that signified a woman's status and identity has also been a hallmark of Asian cultures for centuries. When the Manchu ethnic minority came to power in China in 1644, it forbade women to bind their feet like the majority Han Chinese, whose bound feet connoted feminine refinement and eligibility (see No. 121). Instead, Manchu women wore distinctive high platform shoes that preserved the natural shape of the foot (see Nos. 38, 45). These platforms, possibly influenced

32. Christian Louboutin. "Super Sling Tassel," Spring/Summer 2006

FIG. 19
Attributed to Mu'in Musavvir
(Persian). *Portrait of Shah
Abbas I and a Page*, from
an album, 1632–33. Opaque
watercolor, gold, and silver
on paper, 8⅜ × 4¼ in.
(21.3 × 10.8 cm). Harvard
Art Museums/Arthur M.
Sackler Museum, Gift of
John Goelet, 1960.48. Photo:
Imaging Department
© President and Fellows of
Harvard College

FIG. 20A, B
*Venetian Woman with
Moveable Skirt* (flap
down, bottom; flap lifted,
top). Publisher: Ferrando
Bertelli (Italian, active
Venice, 1561–71). 1563.
Engravings, each sheet:
5½ × 7⁷⁄₁₆ in. (14 × 18.9 cm).
The Metropolitan Museum
of Art, New York, The
Elisha Whittelsey Collection,
The Elisha Whittelsey
Fund, 1955 (55.503.30).
Image copyright © The
Metropolitan Museum
of Art. Image source: Art
Resource, NY

FIG. 21
Tsukioka Yoshitoshi
(Japanese, 1839–1892).
The Moon at Kuruwa, 1886.
Woodblock color print on
paper, sheet: 14 × 9½ in.
(35.6 × 24.1 cm). Brooklyn
Museum, Bequest of Dr.
Eleanor Z. Wallace, 2007.31.7

33 (opposite). Japanese.
Sandals, 1984

by the Western chopine, distinguished the Manchu culturally from the Han. Because the shoes made it difficult to walk, they also replicated the bound foot's halting gait, still considered attractive in Manchu culture.

The Japanese geta, a sandal elevated on wooden teeth that originally kept farmers' feet from sinking into the muddy rice fields, bears a formal resemblance to the *nalin*. Keeping the feet and garments elevated and unpolluted by the ground remained part of the geta's function as it evolved into a sandal worn by priests for religious ceremonies.[2] The geta became a common form of footwear in Japan, but the highest examples were worn by the most elite courtesans (Fig. 21). Both the toothed geta and the solid *pokkuri*, or *okobo*, geta have influenced platform designs by Prada, Winde Rienstra, Vivienne Westwood, Beth Levine, and Noritaka Tatehana (see Nos. 46, 50–53, 55). The split-toe socks traditionally worn with the geta—called *tabi*—have themselves inspired contemporary high heels by Martin Margiela (see No. 48).

As centuries of trade, war, imperial expansion, and tourism have brought encounters between East and West, the Western fascination with foreign or "exotic" fashions has never faltered. Modern designs by Pietro Yantorny and Roger Vivier have borrowed the upturned toes and intricate embroidery and beading of Turkish slippers (see Nos. 41, 42). Rodarte's wedge heels display the distinctive patterns of Ming porcelain, graphic designs in the style of Japanese tattoos cover Jean Paul Gaultier's cantilever-heeled lace-up booties, and Vivier uses the iridescent blue feathers of the white-breasted kingfisher—which adorned clothes and accessories in Imperial China—to decorate his Choc heels (see Nos. 40, 54, 39).[3]

34 (opposite, top). Syrian. Pair of Sandals, 1875–1900*
35 (opposite, bottom). Italian. Chopines, circa 1600
36 (this page). Christian Siriano. Pumps, Fall 2013

37 (opposite). Jean Paul Gaultier. "2-in-1 Wedges," Ready-to-Wear Fall/Winter 2010–11
38 (this page). Chinese. Manchu Woman's Shoe, probably late 19th century

39. Roger Vivier. "Rendez Vous, Limited Edition Blue Feather Choc," Fall/Winter 2013–14
40 (opposite). Rodarte (Kate and Laura Mulleavy). "Ming Printed Leather and Carved Wood Heel," 2011

41. Pietro Yantorny (Italian, 1874–1936). Mule, 1914–19
42 (opposite). Christian Dior (French, 1905–1957). Roger Vivier (French, 1913–1998) for House of Dior. Evening Slippers, 1960

43. Turkish (for Western market). Evening Slippers, 1865–85
44 (opposite). André Perugia (French, 1893–1977) for Paul Poiret (French, 1879–1944). "Le Bal" Slippers, 1924

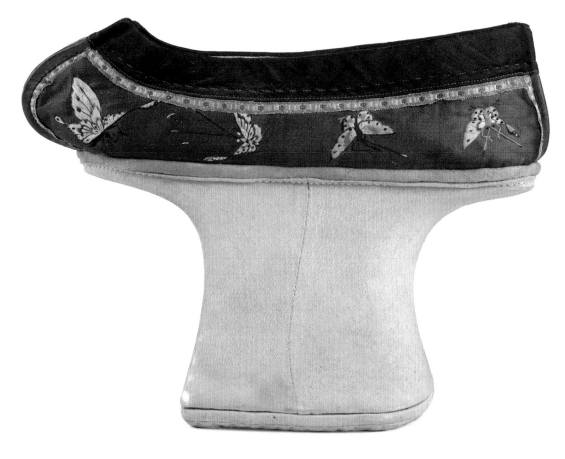

45. Chinese. Manchu Woman's Shoes, probably late 19th century
46 (opposite). Prada. Fuoco Silk and Lizard Platform, Spring/Summer 2013

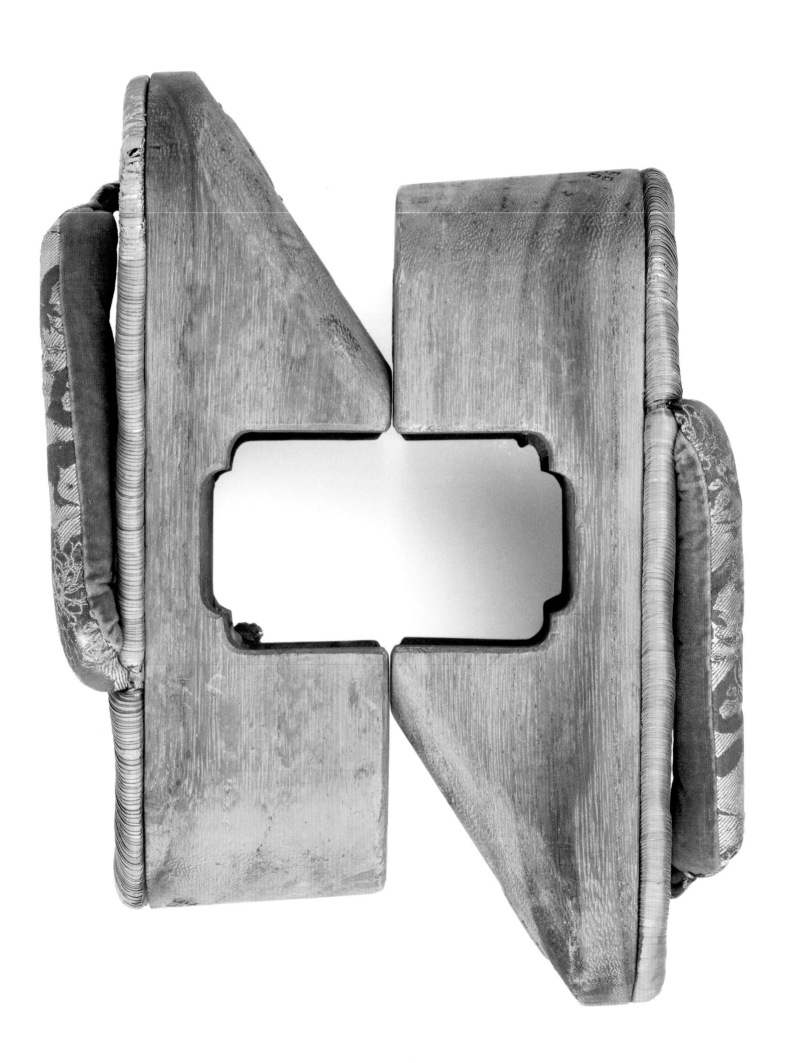

47 (opposite). Japanese. Geta, first half of 20th century
48 (this page). Martin Margiela, Maison Martin Margiela. Pumps, 2001

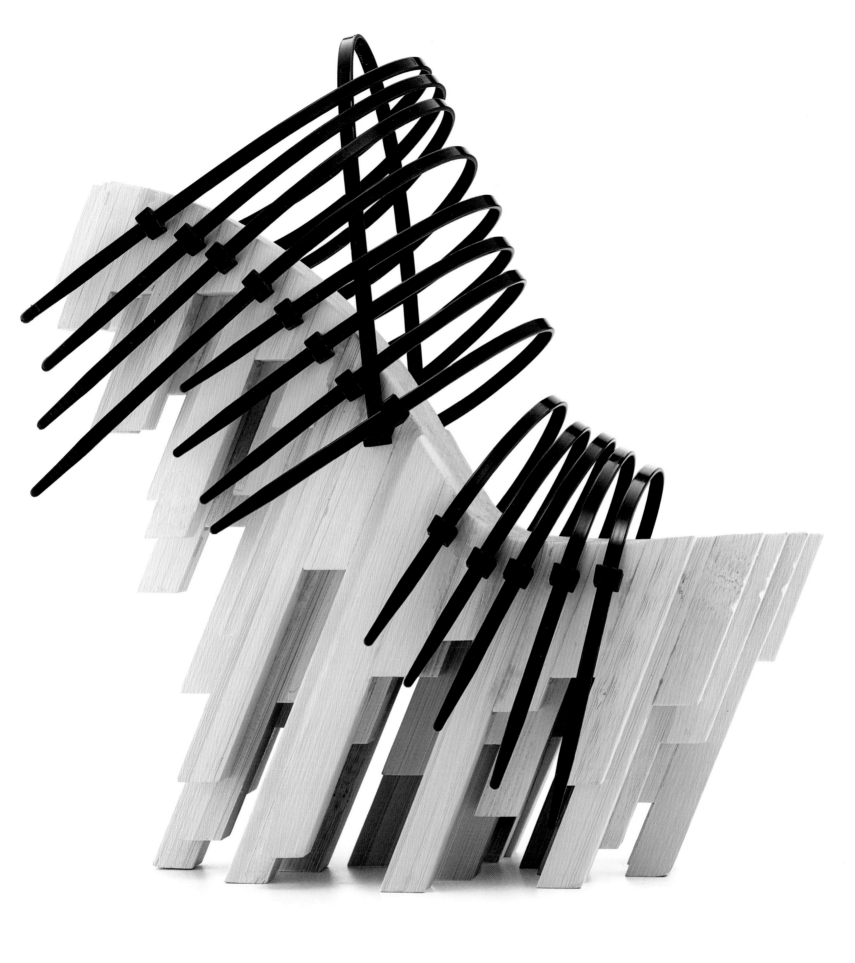

49 (opposite). Walter Steiger. "Ishi Wedge," Spring 2011
50 (this page). Winde Rienstra. "Bamboo Heels," 2012

51 (opposite). Vivienne Westwood. "Rocking Horse Ballerina," 2013 (original design 1985)
52 (this page, top). Beth Levine (American, 1914–2006), Herbert Levine Inc. (American). "Kabuki" Mule, circa 1966
53 (this page, bottom). Beth Levine (American, 1914–2006), Herbert Levine Inc. (American). "Kabuki" Evening Shoe, circa 1965

54. Jean Paul Gaultier. "Nude Tattoo Boots," Ready-to-Wear Spring/Summer 2012

55. Noritaka Tatehana. "Atom," 2012–13
56 (opposite). Christian Louboutin for Manish Malhotra, Platform, 2013

GLAMOUR AND FETISH

Since its invention in the early 1950s, the stiletto has been the ne plus ultra of the high-heeled shoe and the principal sartorial signifier of femininity, as well as of commodified sexuality. Worn by sun-kissed European starlets and American silver-screen goddesses, stilettos are glamour incarnate, whether studded with crystals or covered in flowers (Fig. 22; see also Nos. 63, 72). Tall, slim, and tapered to a sharp point where it meets the ground, the stiletto heel has also long evoked a sense of danger, a link encouraged by its namesake: a slender Italian dagger. Even the clicking sound a stiletto makes as its wearer walks down the street recalls the sound of a switchblade stiletto flicking open. Advertisements, pulp-novel covers, and Hollywood films have helped embed the connection between the sudden and deadly thrust of the knife and the stiletto heel's implied capacity for violence (Fig. 23).[1] Killer heels carry the threat—and promise—of danger and seduction.

The basic form of the stiletto is continually reimagined in ways that play with, and against, the cultural meanings with which it has been invested. Christian Louboutin and Richard Braqo have stripped it down to a thin shaft of metal, revealing the basic structural element inside all stiletto heels that allows them to support the body's weight without breaking (see Nos. 65, 59). These rapier-like heels emphasize the heel as weapon, as does Chau Har Lee's blade heel, which is thin, but

wide like a guillotine (see No. 147). Stilettos can also multiply, mutate, and migrate: Jean Paul Gaultier's ankle strap rises on not one but several stiletto spikes (see No. 66); Tom Ford's wedge is covered with a mass of small thorns (see No. 135), while in one of Iris van Herpen's radical haute couture creations made in collaboration with United Nude, several ominously curved heels rake the ground like claws (see No. 64). In another, spikes line the negative space between heel and sole, conjuring the razor-toothed mouth of a prehistoric sea creature (see No. 67). Even a less pointy heel can be "killer," as model Naomi Campbell discovered when she tumbled down the runway wearing Vivienne Westwood's "Super Elevated Gillies" (see No. 85 and page 4). Despite a slightly lower and wider heel, "Power" pumps by Susan Bennis/Warren Edwards speak for themselves as killer heels, as do flashy pre-stiletto-era tango-style boots (see Nos. 86, 81).

Decorative embellishments and fabrics, such as the revealing fishnet upper on Viktor & Rolf's stiletto, the corsetry detailing on their stiletto mule, or the gold-edged ruffle flourish along the back of Nicholas Kirkwood's imposing black platform pump,

57. Giuseppe Zanotti. Heels, Fall/Winter 2012–13

temper the ferocity of the stiletto heel
(see Nos. 69, 71, 70). Such details suggest
lingerie, symbolically conflating the two
most commonly sexually fetishized women's
garments. Louboutin directly explored
fetishism by creating a series of extreme
heels—not made for walking—that were
photographed by David Lynch (Fig. 24;
also see No. 80).[2] Fetish-style heels like Dolce
& Gabbana's ankle-strap gladiator sandal
(see No. 83)—extremely high, spiky, and
often embellished with buttons, buckles,
studs, straps, or laces—once found only in
specialty shops, have now emerged fully
into mainstream high-heel design, retaining
the erotic frisson of transgression.

FIG. 22 (left)
Allan Grant (American,
1919–2008). Marilyn Monroe
in Ferragamo Heels, 1962.
Photograph. © Allan Grant
(Life Magazine)

FIG. 23 (top, left)
Cover of Richard Marsten,
The Spiked Heel (New York:
Holt, 1956)

FIG. 24 (top, center)
Christian Louboutin
and David Lynch.
Fetish-Ballerine, 2007.
Chromogenic print.
The Irene Lewisohn
Costume Reference Library,
The Costume Institute,
The Metropolitan Museum
of Art, New York. Photo by
David Lynch, courtesy
of Christian Louboutin

58 (top, right). Salvatore
Ferragamo (Italian,
1898–1960). Marilyn
Monroe's Salvatore
Ferragamo Pump, 1959

59 (bottom). Richard Braqo. "Benedetta," 2012
60 (top). Dal Co' (Italian). Pump, 1956

61. Giuseppe Zanotti. Heel, Spring/Summer 2014
62 (opposite). United Nude. "Gaga Shoe," 2012

63. Nicholas Kirkwood. Pumps, Spring/Summer 2013

64 (opposite). Iris van Herpen X United Nude. "Fang," 2012
65 (this page). Christian Louboutin. "Lipspikes Bootie," Fall/Winter 2010–11

66 (opposite). Jean Paul Gaultier. "Mille-Pattes Stilettos," Ready-to-Wear Spring/Summer 1993
67 (this page). Iris van Herpen X United Nude. "Thorn," 2012

68 (opposite). American. Marabou Mule, 1950–59
69 (this page). Viktor & Rolf. Heel, Spring/Summer 2011

70 (opposite). Nicholas Kirkwood. Pumps, Spring/Summer 2013
71 (this page). Viktor & Rolf. Mule, Spring/Summer 2012

72. Brian Atwood. "Sigrid," Spring/Summer 2013
73 (opposite). Charlotte Olympia. "Mae West," Pre-Fall 2013

74. Alexander McQueen. Lace-up Peep Toe Boots, Spring/Summer 2013
75 (opposite). Beth Levine (American, 1914–2006), Herbert Levine Inc. (American). Stocking Shoes, 1953

76 (previous spread). Aoi Kotsuhiroi. "Forbidden Color," 2013

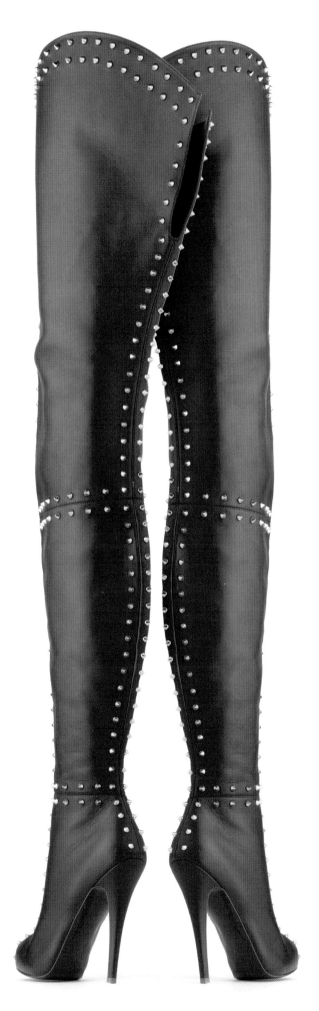

77 (opposite). Maniatis Bottier, Paris. Boots, 1920s
78 (this page). Christian Louboutin. "Metropolis," Fall/Winter 2010–11

79 (opposite). Christian Louboutin. "Big Lips Boots," Fall/Winter 2010–11
80 (this page). Christian Louboutin. Pumps, 2007

81 (bottom). Bray Bros. (American). Evening Boot, circa 1918
82 (top). Bernhard Gronberg (Swedish). Shoe, 1923–29
83 (opposite). Dolce & Gabbana. Sandal, Spring/Summer 2003

84 (opposite). Christian Louboutin. "Printz," Spring/Summer 2013
85 (this page). Vivienne Westwood. "Super Elevated Gillies," 1993

86. Susan Bennis/Warren Edwards. Pumps, circa 1985
87 (opposite). Georgina Goodman. "LOVE," Spring/Summer 2011

ARCHITECTURE

Architecture and shoe design share some concerns: enclosure; protection; harmonized solids, voids, and silhouettes; and a balance of material, form, and function. Structural issues of stress points, loads, and flexion make the comparison even more compelling when it comes to high heels. As heels grew higher and thinner in the eighteenth century, shoemakers experimented with the placement, shape, and angle of the heel to provide stability and reduce the possibility of breakage (see No. 92).

It was not until the 1950s, with the use of extruded steel rods within the heel, that a true skyscraper stiletto could be reliably achieved (see No. 93).[1] This innovation ushered in a new era of architecture-inspired heel placements and shapes, among which the most influential were Roger Vivier's elegant curved "Virgule" and "Choc" heels (see Nos. 94, 96). The architectural impulse is evident in sharp-edged, geometric, graphic heels and platforms by Pierre Hardy, Aperlaï, Atalanta Weller, and Cat Potter that evoke the contours and colors of the modern or futuristic urban skyline (see Nos. 95, 102, 112, 113).

Some high heels borrow architectural elements or motifs: an inverted Eiffel Tower serves as a stiletto for Jean Paul Gaultier in a playful reference to the stiletto's close association with French couture and the tower's soaring steel height, connections that advertisements mined, as well (Fig. 25).

The contours of Miu's Miu's pumps are reminiscent of both the Chrysler Building's Art Deco crown and the stepped construction of an ancient ziggurat (see No. 103). Other more conceptual interfaces between high-heel design and architectural practice include the cantilever configuration, used in bridge and balcony construction. In place of a vertical element at the rear of the shoe, a support extends horizontally like a strut, giving the illusion that the heel of the foot is unsupported. The design looks as futuristic and gravity-defying in contemporary high heels by Marc Jacobs and Rem D. Koolhaas for United Nude (see Nos. 106, 107) as it did when it was first introduced in the early twentieth century (see Fig. 31).

A number of trained architects have brought the specific processes of their discipline to bear directly on high-heel design to create new and unexpected heel typologies: the groundbreaking "Möbius" heel by Koolhaas; Zaha Hadid's striated and dynamically cantilevered "NOVA" heel, which would not appear out of place in a Futurist painting; or Julian Hakes's fluid "Mojito" shoe, whose distinctive shape resulted from examining the biomechanics of the foot (see Nos. 111, 99, 100).

89 (opposite, bottom). Miu Miu. "Nero" Lace-up Platform Heel, Spring/Summer 2008
90 (opposite, top). Enzo Albanese (Italian). Sandal, circa 1958
91 (this page, top). European. Patten, 18th century
92 (this page, bottom). British. Shoe, 1720*

93 (top). Skyscrapers (American). Stiletto, 1955–57
94 (bottom). Roger Vivier. "Virgule Houndstooth," Fall 2014
95 (opposite). Pierre Hardy. "Skyline Heel," Summer 2011

96. Roger Vivier (French, 1913–1998) for House of Dior. Evening Shoe, 1960
97 (opposite). Maison Martin Margiela. "Suspended Demi-Pointe Heel," Spring/Summer 2014

98 (previous spread, left). Tea Petrovic. "Wings/Variation," 2013
99 (previous spread, right). Zaha Hadid X United Nude. "NOVA," 2013

100 (this spread). Julian Hakes. "Mojito," 2012

101 (opposite). Fendi. Heel, 2013
102 (this page). Aperlaï. "Geisha Lines," Fall 2013

103. Miu Miu. "Smeraldo" Leather Pumps, Fall/Winter 2008
104 (opposite). Christian Dior. Heels, Fall 2013

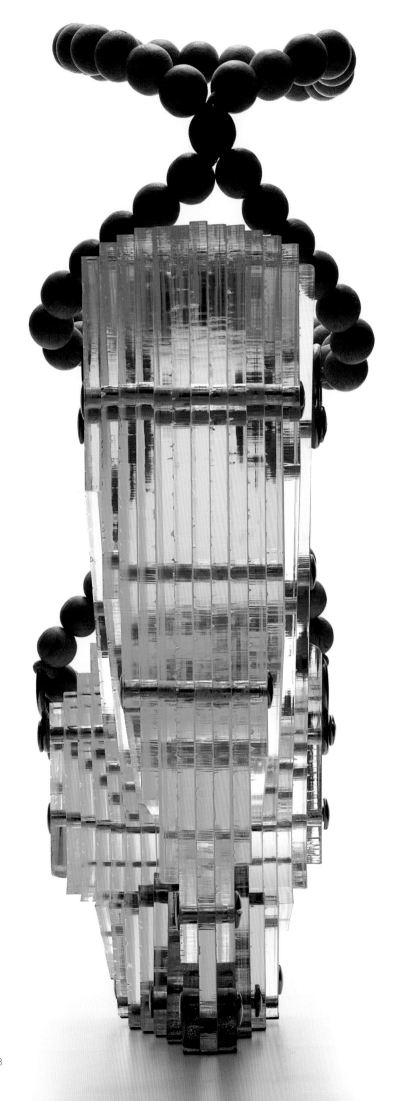

105. Winde Rienstra. "Shutter Heels," 2013

106. Marc Jacobs. Pumps, Spring/Summer 2008
107 (opposite). Rem D. Koolhaas. "Eamz," 2004

108 (top). Delman (American). Shoes, 1938–40
109 (bottom). Victor (American). Platform Sandal, circa 1940
110 (opposite). Balenciaga by Nicolas Ghesquière. Shoes, Fall/Winter 2010. Produced by Balenciaga, Paris

111. Rem D. Koolhaas. "Möbius," 2003
112 (opposite). Atalanta Weller. "The Big Shoes," 2008

113. Cat Potter. "Pernilla, Look 5," 2012

114 (opposite). Projections. Shoes, 1972–76
115 (this page). Balenciaga. Block Heel, Spring 2013

METAMORPHOSIS

The glass slippers in Walt Disney's now-classic *Cinderella*, released in 1950 at the dawn of the stiletto era, featured a high heel (Fig. 26). This was a powerful and popular cultural reinforcement of the long-standing idea that high heels are enchanting and transformative objects. Maison Martin Margiela's glass stilettos played with the strong connection between Cinderella and high heels (No. 116).[1]

The relationship between shoes and physical transformation is perhaps expressed most forcefully and explicitly in the tiny "lotus shoes" worn by Chinese women with bound feet (No. 121). Women who wear high heels also undergo a kind of metamorphosis, however. Not only do they appear taller, but their entire posture changes. The chest is thrust forward, the derriere is lifted, and the leg appears longer, the calf more taut and rounded, and the foot smaller. These body modifications, though temporary, create the distinctive silhouette and gait that for centuries and in different cultures have signified alluring femininity and stimulated the erotic imagination.[2] It is a posture that has also been ridiculed, as in an American song from 1868, when high heels were back in style after a long period of fashionable flats (Fig. 27):

The Ladies wanting something new,
 as women are so prone to do,
Wear lofty heels upon the shoe to
 give them a Grecian Bend.
With foot so short and heel so high they
 can't stand plumb if they would try,
And so they think to catch the eye by
 means of the Grecian Bend.[3]

A century later, the artist duo ANTONIO also took these modifications to the extreme in a series of *Shoe Metamorphosis* drawings, in which a woman in heels is herself transformed into a stiletto (Fig. 28).

While all high heels are agents of transformation, some appear to be undergoing a metamorphosis themselves, with designs that emphasize flux, transition, or hybrid forms. Iris van Herpen's mass of sinuous, interwoven tendrils reaching toward the ground evokes the classical nymph Daphne, whose feet became roots as she was transformed into a laurel tree (see No. 124). Heels by Kerrie Luft and Prada spiral into leaves or flowers (see Nos. 129, 130). The sole of Beth Levine's shoe coils around itself to form a heel, and JANTAMINIAU stretches the high heel to the exaggerated proportions of a mutation in progress (see Nos. 125, 143). "Heliotrope," by René van den Berg and Karin Janssen, references the sun's power to transform, curving around and in on itself, until only a memory of the high-heel form remains (see No. 117).

Some metamorphic or hybridized designs are informed by the shocking or humorous juxtapositions of Surrealism: the stiletto's edges and sharp points are blurred and softened in Céline's fur-covered version (see No. 127); Miu Miu's patent Mary Jane heels are part teacup (see No. 126). Elsa Schiaparelli transformed a black high heel into a hat, a symbolic reordering of the body that brought the fetish object of the sexual gaze up to eye level (see No. 118 and Fig. 11). In his "Déjà vu" slingbacks, Christian Louboutin puts eyes back on the high heel—literally—where they meet and return the fetishizing gaze (see No. 119).

High heels can evoke the attributes of an animal, as seen in the sleek plumage covering Yves Saint Laurent's stiletto or in the fantastical ferocity of Walter Steiger's "Unicorn Tayss" or Louboutin's "Puck" (see Nos. 134, 139, 142). Such designs conjure trophies of the hunt, and recall how the earliest humans adorned their bodies with animal skins and feathers, frequently performing transformational rituals while wearing them. Other designs, such as Alexander McQueen's "Armadillo" heel or Leanie van der Vyver's purposefully impossible "Scary Beautiful" heels, suggest the metamorphosis of the foot *into* an animal's foot (Figs. 29, 30). Martin Margiela's cloven-toed heels, Noritaka Tatehana's hooflike platforms, and Iris Schieferstein's heels made from actual horse hooves and bones (see Nos. 48, 55, 131) all seem to fulfill the observations made by a comparative anatomist in 1781: "Wealthy women walk . . . by reason of the height of their heels, on the fore-ends of their feet, and consequently, very badly; they walk . . . like the majority of quadrupeds—on their toes only."[4]

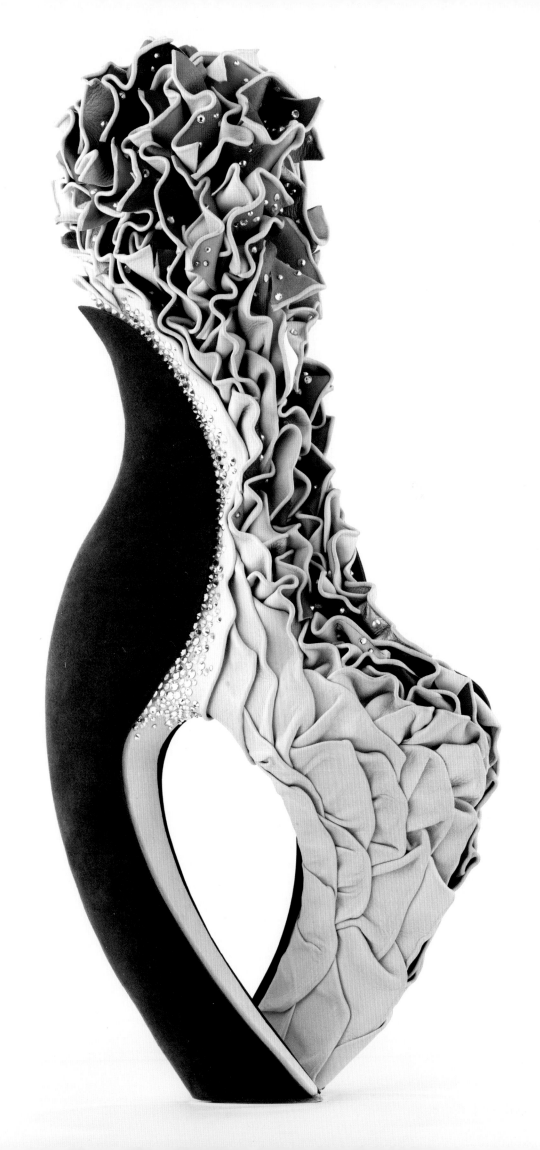

118 (opposite). Elsa Schiaparelli (Italian, 1890–1973). Shoe Hat, Winter 1937–38
119 (this page). Christian Louboutin. "Déjà vu," Fall/Winter 2011–12

120 (opposite). Céline. "Trompe L'oeil Pump," 2013
121 (this page). Chinese. Shoe for Women's Bound Feet, 19th century

122 (opposite). Aperlaï. "Pico Hands," Fall/Winter 2013–14
123 (this page). Helmut Lang. Shoes, Spring/Summer 2003

124. Iris van Herpen X United Nude. "Beyond Wilderness," 2013

125. Beth Levine (American, 1914–2006), Herbert Levine Inc. (American). Slingback Shoe, circa 1962
126 (opposite). Miu Miu. "Ortensia and Oro" Platform Lace-up Heel, Spring/Summer 2008

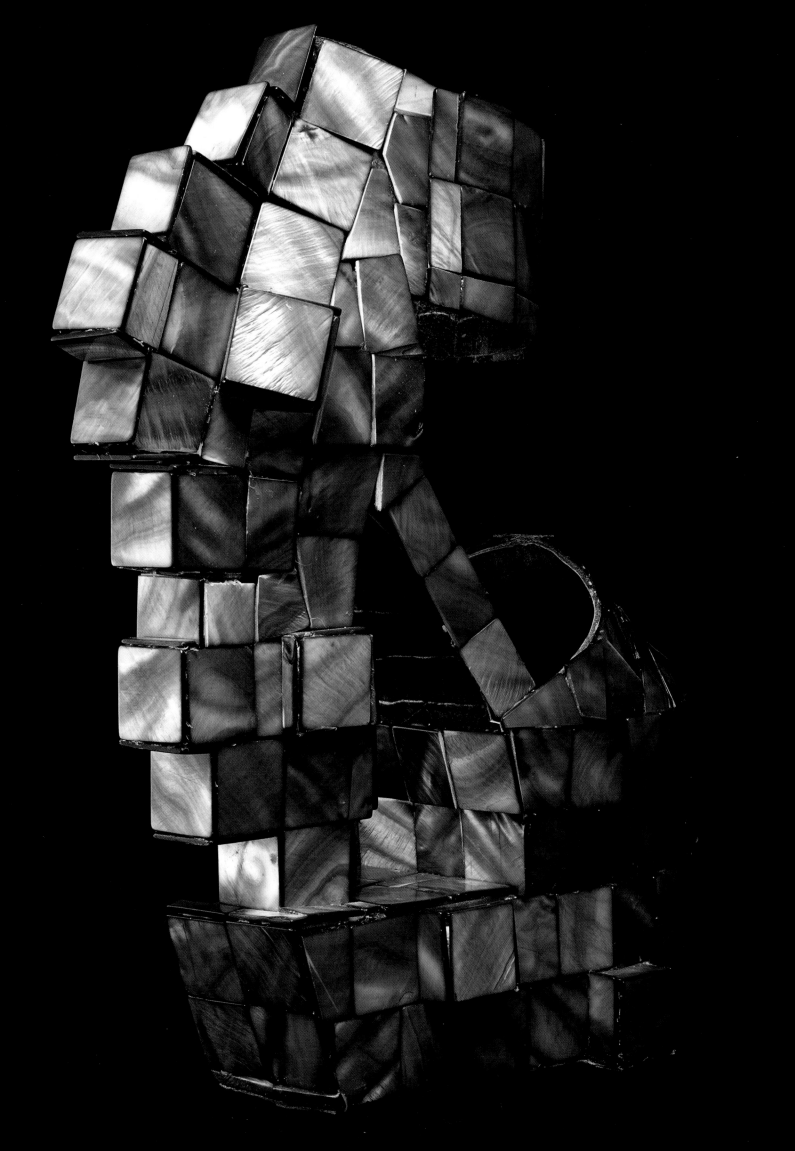

127 (previous spread, left). Céline. "Fur Pump," Spring 2013
128 (previous spread, right). Shoise (Matilda Maroti and Petra Högström). "Mother of Pearl," 2013

129 (opposite). Kerrie Luft. "Thandie," 2013
130 (this page). Prada. Sandal in Cipria and Cordovan Leather, Spring/Summer 2008

131. Iris Schieferstein. "Horse Shoes 3," 2006
132 (opposite). Maison Martin Margiela. Boot, Spring/Summer 2012

133 (next spread). Masaya Kushino. "Stairway to Heaven," 2013

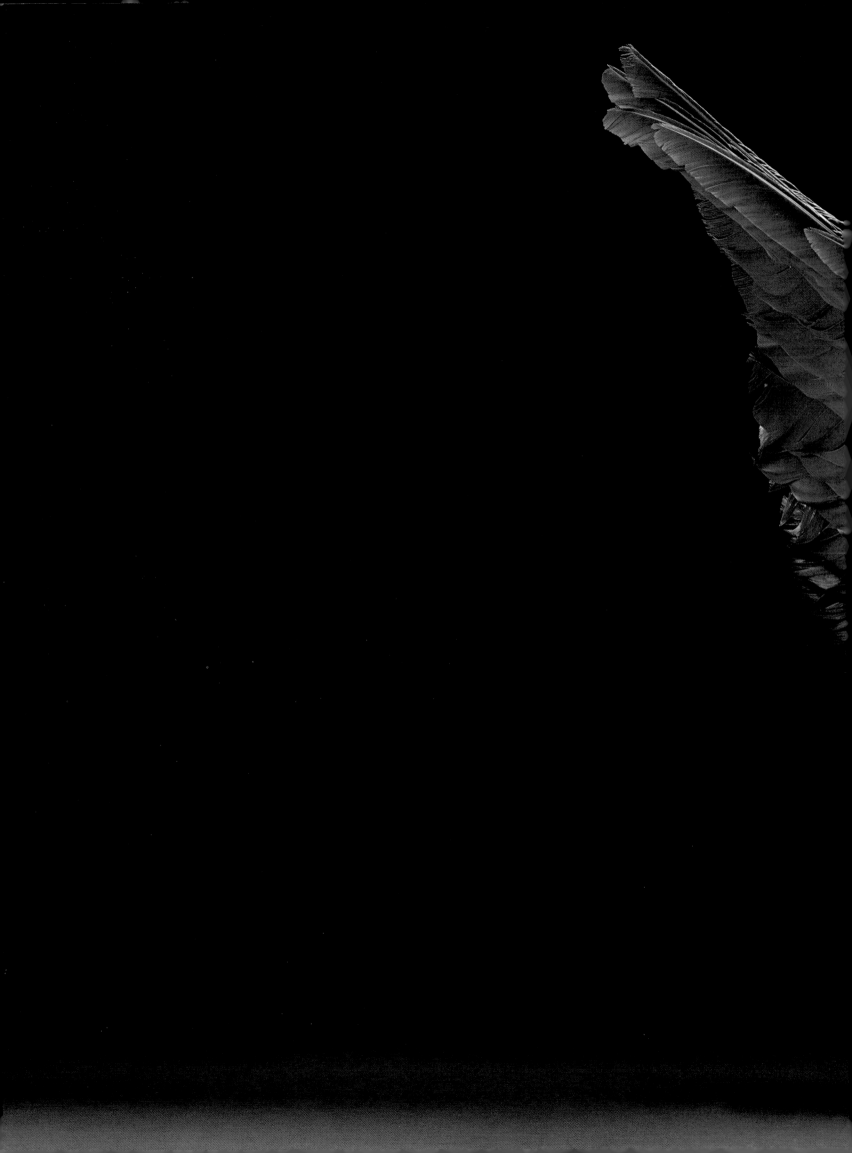

134. Yves Saint Laurent (French, 1936–2008). Yves Saint Laurent Rive Gauche. Shoe, 2004
135 (opposite). Tom Ford. Wedge Shoes, Spring 2013

136. Isabel Canovas. Pump. Fall/Winter 1988–89

137 (opposite, top). House of Dior for Delman. Designed by Roger Vivier (French, 1913–1998). Evening Shoe, 1954

138 (opposite, bottom). Steven Arpad (French, 1904–1999). "Model No. 256" Shoe Prototype, 1939

139. Walter Steiger. "Unicorn Tayss," Spring 2013

140 (top). Fendi. Bootie, 2013
141 (bottom). Masaya Kushino. "Chimera," 2011
142 (opposite). Christian Louboutin. "Puck," Fall/Winter 2011–12

143 (next spread). JANTAMINIAU. "Tarnished Beauty," 2012. (Handcrafted by René van den Berg)

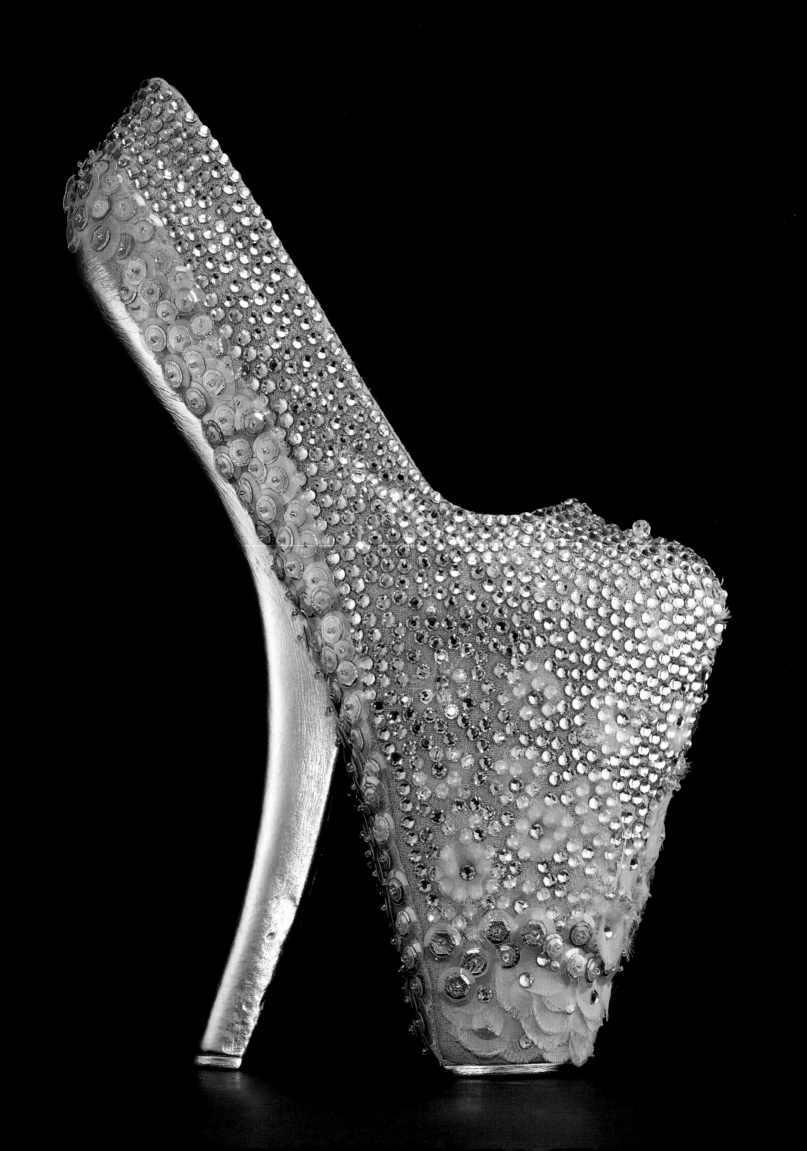

SPACE
WALK

FIG. 31
Still from British Pathé
newsreel *Eve, AD
2000!,* March 20,
1939. The British Pathé
Archive, London, UK,
1184.16 #37. Image:
© British Pathé LTD.

144 (opposite). Rem D.
Koolhaas. "Flat Pack
Shoe (for Moon Life
Project)," 2010

Shoes have long been symbolic of journeys, flight, and speed. Although it is arguably difficult to walk far or fast in them, high heels have frequently emphasized this association, and their growing popularity in the early twentieth century coincided with the introduction of rockets, aerosol cans, nylon, and other harbingers of a sleek and dynamic future (Figs. 31, 32). Since then, cutting-edge design and fabrication technologies, new and unconventional materials, and a range of references, from space travel and science fiction to robotics and cyborgs, have helped designers imagine the future in high heels (Fig. 33).

Salvatore Ferragamo's iconic 1947 "Invisible" sandal, a curved wedge heel with an upper formed by a single strand of nylon filament, combined innovative materials with a minimalist aesthetic (see No. 148). The influence of its light, aerodynamic style and emphasis on transparency continues to be seen in futuristic designs like Tamar Areshidze's "Walking on Water" sandal, which rests on a platform of curved organic glass, Chau Har Lee's Perspex wedge, Givenchy's cone heel with clear PVC upper, and Rem D. Koolhaas's modular "Flat Pack Shoe," created as part of a project to design products for traveling and living in space (see Nos. 149, 162, 145, 144).

Streamlined jet-age design influenced the popular midcentury "Satellite" Jumping Shoe (see No. 151)—the children's version of a futuristic elevated shoe—as well as Prada's retro-futuristic mules ornamented with 1950s-style car taillights and its flame-heeled wedges (see Nos. 150, 165).

Fashion truly went into orbit in the 1960s, when the new reality of space travel inspired André Courrèges and Pierre Cardin to create bold, geometric fashions. Although the go-go boots of that era had lower heels, their space-age aesthetic is nonetheless still apparent in high heels such as Manolo Blahnik's mod stiletto boots designed in collaboration with the artist Damien Hirst and FINSK's gravity-defying color-blocked platforms (see Nos. 152, 169). High heels by Zaha Hadid, Andreia Chaves, Victoria Spruce, Zuzana Serbak, and threeASFOUR achieve the fluid or faceted shapes suggestive of spacecraft and interstellar travel by using new 3-D printing or rotational molding techniques and high-tech materials such as carbon fiber and plastics (see Nos. 99, 146, 158–60).

These high-heel designs, as well as others by Rosanne Bergsma, Giuseppe Zanotti, and Atalanta Weller (see Nos. 157, 167, 168), resemble machine parts or futuristic, retro-futuristic, or steampunk augmentations, armatures, or prostheses associated with robots or cyborgs.[1] Sputniko! and Masaya Kushino designed a mechanized high heel in response to the recent Fukushima nuclear disaster. Called "Healing Fukushima," the shoes contain seeds of a plant known to absorb radioactive substances from the soil (see No. 163). As one walks in them, the seeds are automatically planted in the ground, directly connecting the high heel to the nuclear promise and danger that have characterized visions of the future for more than seventy years.

FIG. 32
Models demonstrating nylons for the crowds at New York World's Fair, 1939. © E. I. du Pont de Nemours & Company. Hagley Digital Images. Hagley Museum and Library, Wilmington, Delaware, 1969.001

FIG. 33
Still from Sputniko! (British/Japanese, born Japan, 1985). *The Moonwalk Machine—Selena's Step*, 2013. Installation with video (color, sound), screens, and lambda print, 4 min. 30 sec., dimensions variable. © Sputniko! Courtesy the artist and Scai the Bathhouse, Tokyo. Photo: Rai Royal

145 (opposite). Givenchy by Riccardo Tisci. Heel, Women's Ready-to-Wear Spring/Summer 2013

146. Andreia Chaves. Invisible "Naked Version," 2011, Invisible Shoe Series

147. Chau Har Lee. "Blade Heel," 2010

148. Salvatore Ferragamo (Italian, 1898–1960). "Invisible" Sandal, 1947*
149 (opposite). Tamar Areshidze. "Walking on Water," 2012

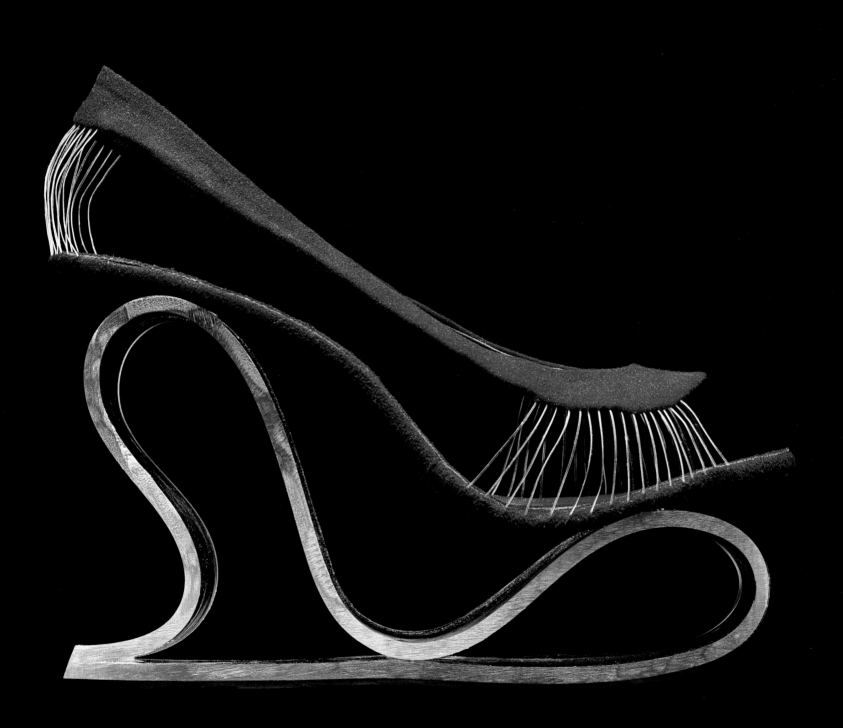

150 (opposite). Prada. Leather Sandal in Mango, Sabbia, and Palissandro Leather, Spring/Summer 2012

151 (this page). Rapaport Brothers, Inc. (American). "Satellite" Jumping Shoe, circa 1955

152. Damien Hirst (designer). Manolo Blahnik (manufacturer). "Dot" Boots, 2002
153 (opposite). Terry de Havilland. Boots, 1979–81

154 (opposite). Conspiracy/Gianluca Tamburini. "Aerial Mardi Gras," 2013
155 (this page). Chanel. "Light Bulb Heel," 2008, "Paris London" Métiers d'Art Collection

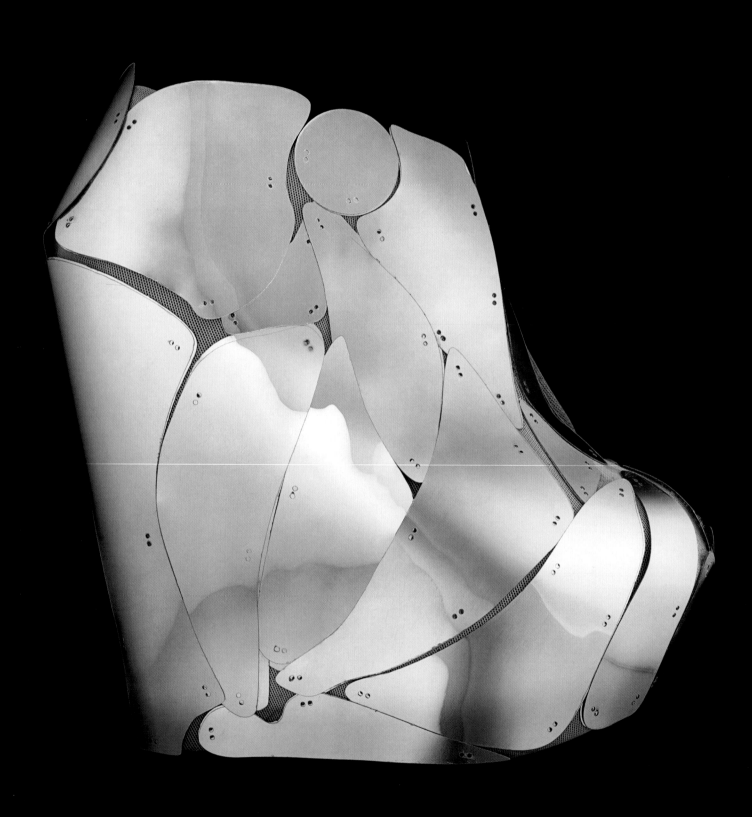

156 (previous spread, left). threeASFOUR (Gabriel Asfour, Adi Gil, Angela Donhauser). "Mirror Wedge," 2013
157 (previous spread, right). Rosanne Bergsma. Heel, 2011

158 (opposite). Victoria Spruce. Wedge, 2012
159 (this page). Zuzana Serbak. Heels, 2011

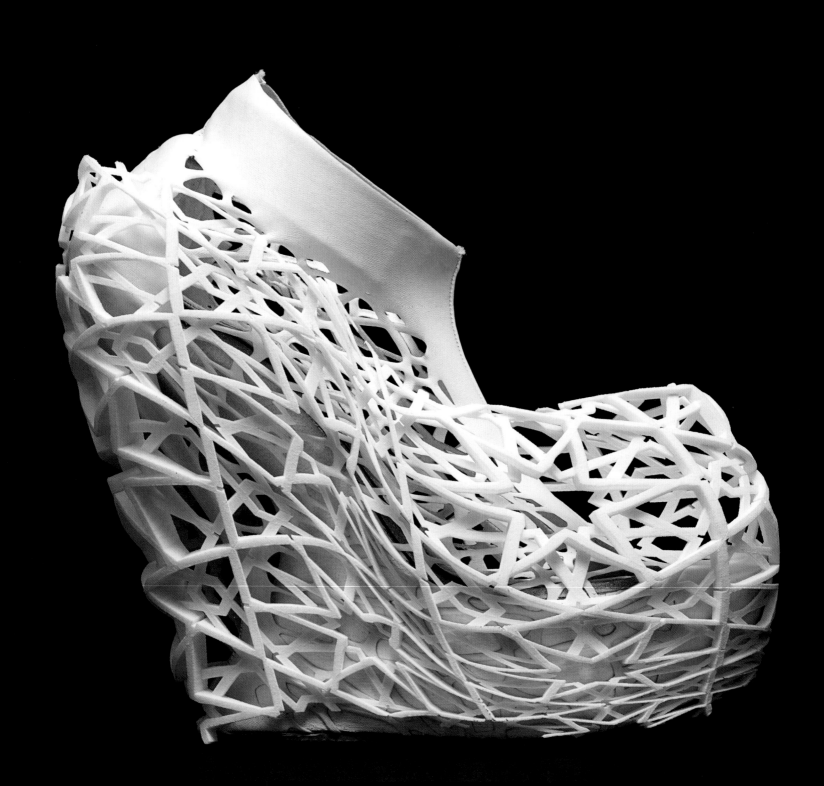

160 (previous spread, left). threeASFOUR (Gabriel Asfour, Adi Gil, Angela Donhauser). "3-D-Printed Wedge," 2013
161 (previous spread, right). Nicholas Kirkwood. Wedge, Spring/Summer 2013

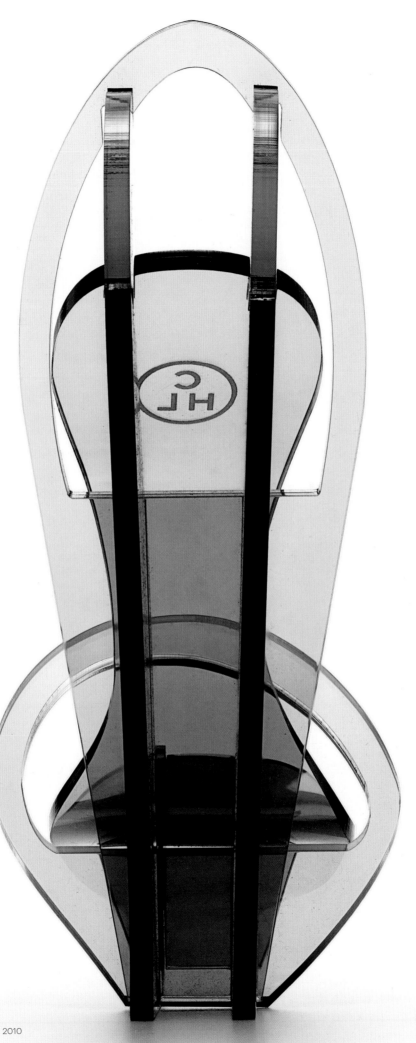

162 (this spread). Chau Har Lee. Platform, 2010

163 (opposite). Sputniko!. "Healing Fukushima (Nanohana Heels)," 2012. Shoe design by Masaya Kushino
164 (this page). JANTAMINIAU. "L'Image Tranquille," 2013. (Handcrafted by René van den Berg)

165. Prada. Wedge Sandal in Rosso, Bianco, and Nero Leather, Spring/Summer 2012

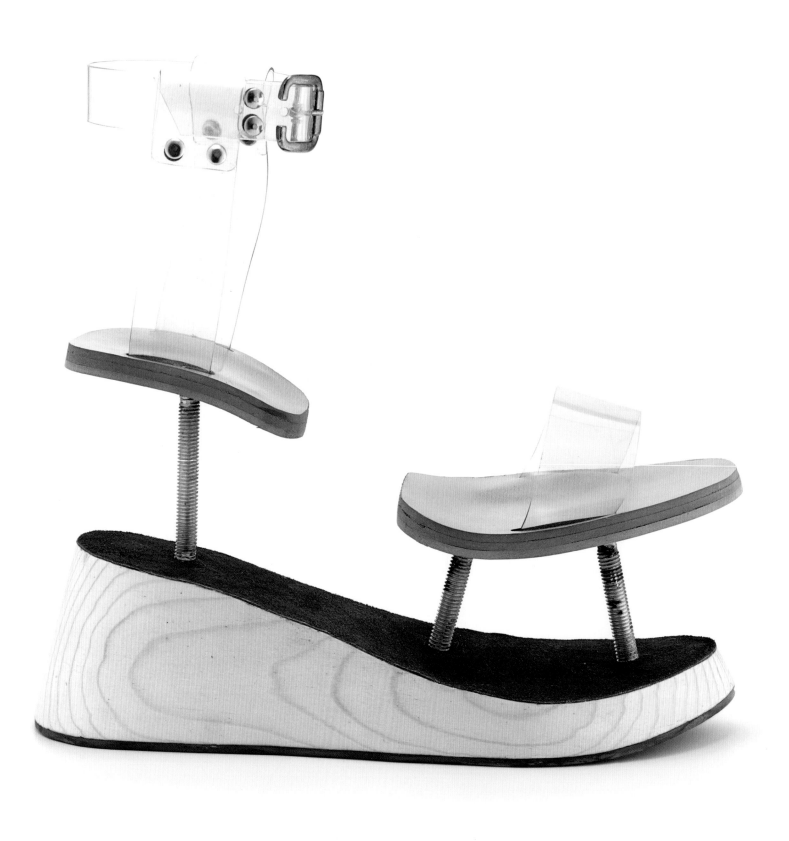

166. Tamar Areshidze. "Levitating Shoe," 2011
167 (opposite). Giuseppe Zanotti. "Gladiator Boot," Spring/Summer 2013

168. Atalanta Weller. "The Woven Poodle Shoes," 2009
169 (opposite). FINSK. "Project 3," 2010

FILMS

For the exhibition *Killer Heels: The Art of the High-Heeled Shoe*, the Brooklyn Museum commissioned six original short films that take the high heel as a conceptual starting point. These provocative films, by the artists Ghada Amer and Reza Farkhondeh, Zach Gold, Steven Klein, Nick Knight, Marilyn Minter, and Rashaad Newsome, explore the cult status of the high-heeled shoe and its roles in discourses of fantasy, power, and identity, as well as its high profile in visual culture.

GHADA AMER AND REZA FARKHONDEH

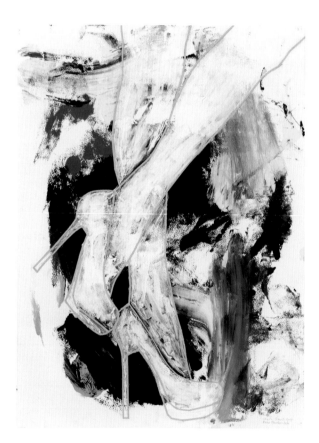

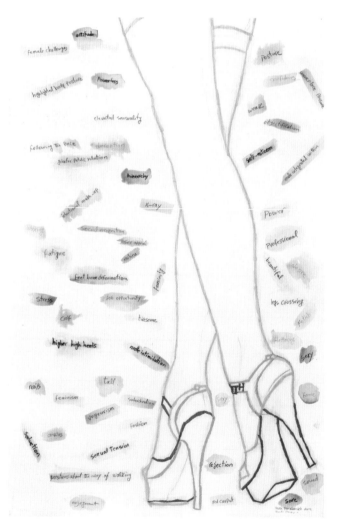

170 (above). Ghada Amer and Reza Farkhondeh. *A Pause in An Abstract Painting*, 2014. Preparatory drawing for the film *Higher Me* (working title). Acrylic, pencil, tape, and gel medium on paper, 29¾ × 22 in. (75.6 × 55.9 cm). Courtesy of the artists. Photo: Brian Buckley

FIG. 34 (right) Reza Farkhondeh and Ghada Amer. *In Step*, 2014. Pencil, graphite, tape, and gel medium on paper, 40 x 26 in. (101.6 x 66 cm). Courtesy of the artists. Photo: Brian Buckley

171. Zach Gold. Sketch
for the video installation
4 Screens, 2014. Courtesy
of Zach Gold

ZACH GOLD

I want to tell stories that don't exist.

Screenshots, highlighted phrases, GIFs, short
video, and hazy memories indicate the presence
of stories that never completely exist, but continue
to suggest, and influence us.

I am interested in the compulsion we have
to create stories. We are compelled to surround
these abbreviated inputs with something more
comprehensive. The way you expand on the first
few sentences of a bedtime story before you
drift off to sleep.

Fashion works with suggestion in a similar way.
Designers interject short, saturated blasts of
aesthetic information into the world every season,
signaling untold narratives. It is left for us to finish
the story. If the archetypes of human storytelling
exist within us, why not just give a glimpse,
a few details, a single scene? Let the rest of the
story tell itself. —ZACH GOLD

STEVEN KLEIN

Women are more often targets of the whims of fashion designers than men, and in recent times women's shoes have reached the apex of the unnatural. It has been said throughout time that "one must suffer to be beautiful," and it is well known that high heels can cause spinal damage and other physical problems. In this film, a woman wearing high heels walks over the body of a man—the feminine dominating the masculine through a fashion device, giving the pain of the unnatural back to the man. It imagines a kind of revenge taken by women who have been offered the bondage of unnatural postures created through mass-market fabrications. —STEVEN KLEIN

172. Storyboard for
Steven Klein's film *Untitled,
791*, 2014. Courtesy of
Steven Klein Studio,
© Steven Klein, 2014

NICK KNIGHT

The glass slipper in fairy tales has become a leitmotif for the painful pursuit of love. It is a symbol that embodies both profound beauty and implicit violence. While at first glance incredibly seductive, the shoe is uncomfortable to wear and presents the constant peril that the glass will smash and sever the skin. The film plays with this fetishistic emblem, creating a story of extreme fragility and danger. Passion, tension, hardship, and discomfort are all themes that underlie this exploration of shoes and their natural associations with excess and desire. —NICK KNIGHT

173. Nick Knight. Study for
the film *La Douleur Exquise*,
2014. Courtesy of Nick
Knight and SHOWstudio

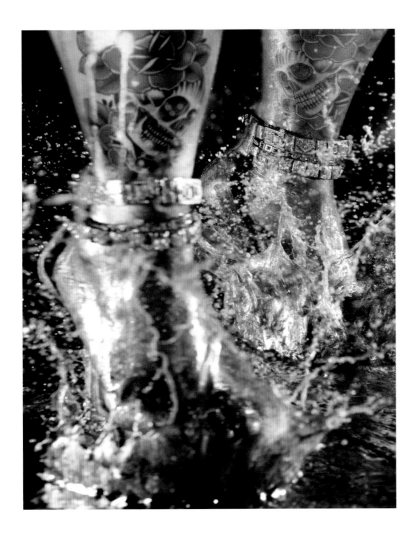

MARILYN MINTER

My work, whether using painting, photography, or video, thrives and focuses on the moment where clarity becomes abstraction and beauty meets the grotesque. Continuing my forty-year examination of glamour and its underbelly, I've recently turned my focus to the physical material and space between the camera and my subject, whether it is suspended liquid splashes, a pane of glass, or deteriorated graffiti. My images are voracious, and ambiguity is always present.

My new video concentrates on the action and interplay between the subject, a trained dancer, and the metallic liquid seeping onto the set. The video will employ different speeds, from ultra–slow motion to the normal 24 frames per second. The camera lens will move within this atmospheric space, focusing on close-up magnifications of splashing liquid and the subject's legs as she dances. The dancer will wear high heels as she moves in and through the constantly accumulating puddle of silver.   —MARILYN MINTER

174. Marilyn Minter. Study for the video *Smash*, 2014. Courtesy of the artist and Salon 94, New York

RASHAAD NEWSOME

The video *Knot* combines my interest in knot theory, the performative language of the house dance style known as "Vogue Fem," the design formulas of heraldry, and Baroque architecture. Knot theory, a branch of geometric topology, studies the embedding of circles into three-dimensional space. The hand movements, referred to as Hand Performance, that compose the main elements of Vogue Fem are loosely based on a figure eight, or Listing's knot.

The video presents an abstracted, collaged environment informed by the designs of Baroque architecture and created out of so-called Veblen goods: commodities such as designer high heels that, because of their exclusivity and appeal as status symbols, are in increased demand as their price increases. Against this environment, abstracted and multiplied figures outfitted in their finest armor dance, sing, sparkle, and morph to an original sound score, creating knotlike forms that are reminiscent of armorial achievements or full heraldic displays.   —RASHAAD NEWSOME

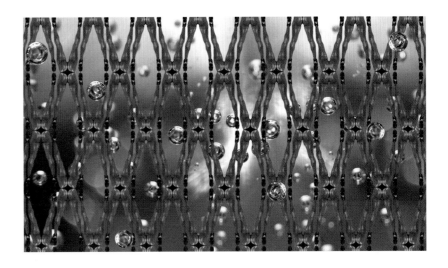

175. Rashaad Newsome. Still from the video installation *Knot*, 2014. Courtesy of the artist

SPEAKING OF HEELS

BECOMING A HIGH-HEEL DESIGNER

GABRIEL ASFOUR, ADI GIL, AND ANGELA DONHAUSER (threeASFOUR): In the past we collaborated with several brands and used their existing styles to fit in our collections until we realized that we needed to have our own heels. The shoe accessories called *jambières* that we used over boots for our Fall/Winter 2012 collection got a lot of attention, so for our Spring/Summer 2013 collection we decided to customize our own shoe: the "Mirror Mirror Shoe."

BRIAN ATWOOD: I got my start in shoes quite by accident. I was designing clothes for Gianni Versace in Italy. On a whim he asked me to design some shoes for the Versace haute couture show. I had never really designed shoes before that. As it turned out, my shoes (super-high heels) were well received, and from there my path as a shoe designer began.

ZAHA HADID: I've always been fascinated by shoes. I adore high heels. Twenty years ago I wore the most uncomfortably high-heeled shoes but I've become a little more practical with age, and don't wear them so often anymore. I'm into fashion and shoes because they contain the mood of the day, of the moment—like music, literature, and art—whereas architecture is a very long process from the start of a project to its completion.

JULIAN HAKES: I had no family or friends in high places, no experience in footwear design, and no connections in the industry. I was simply exploring an idea and a strong feeling that there was something new to be discovered.

Nicholas Kirkwood. Wedge, Spring/Summer 2013 (No. 161)

I was also actually very frustrated with architecture at that time. I don't quite know why, but it felt right to make my own rules and to invest time in my own ideas. I started on a number of innovative new projects including investigating fashion and footwear. There was a strong theme running through these projects: to create projects for today with today's materials and technology and not to rely on, or be swayed by, the way things had been done before. I made the original "Mojito" shoe by wrapping my own foot with tracing paper and masking tape, and drawing shapes on my foot. The moment I cut the shape away from my foot I knew there was something new. I posted early concept images to a design blog, and the response was amazing—people from all over the world asked me to develop the designs into a walkable, workable shoe. I guess it was like early crowd-sourced fashion design.

PIERRE HARDY: I worked many years as a fashion illustrator, and seeing that it was "easy" for me to draw almost anything, someone proposed that I design shoes.

REM D. KOOLHAAS (UNITED NUDE): I'm the typical fool who got suckered into doing something foolish for love. I started designing my first high heels for a girl who broke my heart. I came up with the "Möbius" back in 1999 while still studying in the Netherlands. I was scaling down architecture to its smallest and most vulnerable scale. I was just about to start my thesis project for my MA in architecture, so I integrated the shoes into my project to make sure I didn't waste any time. The "Möbius" made me change my profession and made me move to the other side of the world: it was the shoe that I made, but also the shoe that made me.

CHAU HAR LEE: I have always loved making things and my family encouraged me to pursue my creative interests, so I studied art and learned how to apply my skills. Footwear seemed to be the perfect blend of sculpture and textiles, which led me to get a BA at Cordwainers College and later an MA in Footwear Design at the Royal College of Art in London. I enjoy

the challenge of designing high heels and working out the combination and balance of technical and aesthetic considerations.

CHRISTIAN LOUBOUTIN: If you have an interest/love for shoes, not necessarily from the perspective of fashion, but more of how shoes influence your body language and your attitude, then I think it is natural to be drawn to high heels because they truly transform a woman's body.

JULIA LUNDSTEN (FINSK): Like most girls, I always loved interesting, beautiful shoes, but the actual journey to becoming a shoe designer was based on more factors. I grew up in a family with architect parents, so looking at details, shapes, and architectural structures has always been very natural for me. I studied Womenswear for my BA degree, and I was always mostly interested in the more structural side of pattern cutting as well as materials and details, rather than draping on the body. I decided to apply for an MA in Footwear Design at the Royal College of Art. When I got into footwear design properly, I instantly knew this would be the right balance of structural design and fashion. So I suppose I came into shoe design thanks to a combination of interest in design and other influences, rather than a childhood dream of becoming a shoe designer.

WINDE RIENSTRA: For my first fashion show at Amsterdam Fashion Week I was looking for shoes that would go with my collection. Since my collections are more like sculpture, on the border between clothing and object, fashion and art, I couldn't find anything that would go with the collection. I had no idea how to make shoes, so I bought some heels and covered them completely in wooden scales. I wanted to design heels to be the finishing touch of my clothing collections—an extra element that could surprise the audience and bring the whole collection and concept of the collection to a higher level. After the first heels, I made the heels for my second collection from scratch; I wanted them to be authentic and completely my design.

BRIAN ATWOOD: Brancusi is a big inspiration. His sculptures are tall and elongated, and their frequent use of metal fabrications make them shiny and eye-catching. Other artists who always are a source of inspiration include Helmut Newton and Chris von Wangenheim, who almost invariably in their work had gorgeous women in heels, sometimes wearing nothing else. Charles Jourdan's ads from the seventies are also iconic. Eric Stanton, an illustrator, took bondage and fantasy to a fantastic, beautiful place, since shoes fascinated him. Even Allen Jones's fetish furniture that featured thigh-high stilettos incorporated into chairs and tables pops into my mind now and again as I am sketching.

I have an archive of over five thousand shoes that is my go-to reference when designing. When I look at a vintage shoe, the reference that inspires me may be a small detail like an eyelet, or I may use the entire concept such as a chic pair of patchwork boots. The art of designing is putting my unique stamp on all of this.

Exotic and high heels are synonymous. It's why skins from crocodile, snake, and ostrich are so often used in the material of the most coveted shoes. Similarly, references to exotic places make the allure of high heels more mysterious and aspirational. If you can't travel to a faraway place, your shoes can take you there—at least in your state of mind.

PIERRE HARDY: Sometimes a very specific material or color will be the starting point of a story in the collection. Sometimes it is a whole moment, period, or mood that gives the sense to a collection. But often it is the meeting, the mixing, the collage, the crossing of some very tiny precise details with a more global mood that builds the spirit of a collection. Strangely, the most abstract or conceptual artists are the most influential to me—Sol LeWitt, Donald Judd, Brice Marden, Dan Graham. And at the opposite end, the classics, for a certain expression of femininity: Botticelli, Caravaggio, the French eighteenth century.

Even if I don't quote the history of fashion intentionally, history and fashion history are a part of our culture. Actually, I hope that this culture does "resonate" with my work (or vice versa). I only hope that I don't "echo" it. Once a certain form of beauty has been achieved, at any time, in any culture, we want to recreate it, as an ultimate achievement of femininity, but with modern means. But the archetype remains.

I don't think heels are more extreme now than they used to be during the Venetian Renaissance, for example. It is just "waves." The only limit to the height is the fall.

MASAYA KUSHINO: I need the space and height because I use material that has a lot of volume. High heels stimulate my imagination and creativity like a switch. I see a high heel, and I imagine what it can be. . . .

I live in Kyoto, where there are many old temples and buildings with beautiful details that inspire me. I'm most inspired by historical artifacts, craft, and traditional techniques. I saw an exhibition that showcased the Japanese emperor's art and old artifacts—I loved the details and the luxurious materials, such as gold, pearl, and special wood, that were used to make these objects, which are really high quality and take a lot of time to produce. They are not for daily use. My shoes are not for daily use, necessarily. I want to leave something behind that is special and is worth remembering.

Sometimes the heel or the form of a shoe I've seen really captivates me. I'm not necessarily conscious that I am using these forms in my work, but they definitely impact me.

ALESSANDRA LANVIN (APERLAÏ): Artists such as Miró, Pollock, Picasso, and Mondrian, and, for the structures, architects Ron Arad and Ettore Sottsass . . . all nourish my creations.

The Japanese tradition, Katharine Hepburn, androgynous men's moccasins, Sophia Loren in the fifties, are all mythic figures and/or scenarios. Reinterpretation is the power to transform the myth and make it still live in the collective imagination but in a modern way.

CHAU HAR LEE: I can be inspired by a combination of things, from a conversation to an exhibition or a material, object, or book—things that might accumulate over time to form some kind of narrative. I love to see a story unfolding. Occasionally this can be something spontaneous and immediate, or it could take a long time to research and develop. I try not to look at other shoes in order to not become too heavily influenced.

CHRISTIAN LOUBOUTIN: Everything I see or touch, whether I like it or dislike it, has some kind of influence, or at least a resonance, in my work. Images make an imprint on the brain, whether a light, direct, or unconscious one.

When it comes to high heels, the first person who comes to mind is Allen Jones. Also Bettie Page in the 1950s is very important.

JULIA LUNDSTEN (FINSK): I'm very inspired by details and shapes in architecture and furniture design. Different cultures and traditional ways of making shoes inspire me, but I implement these techniques in a very different, modern way that suits my aesthetic. I respect traditional crafts that have been passed down from generation to generation, while materials themselves and their own unique characteristics are also a source of inspiration. I also get inspired by contrasts, such as a very polished, finished surface of a heel combined with a more rustic natural leather upper, or by the contrasts of busy London life compared to the very quiet, calm Finnish landscapes and a much slower pace of life.

I once got into a very heated discussion with a jewelry designer who had a really black-and-white view about how jewelry design can be art but shoe design cannot. She argued that shoes are worn and therefore have a function, whereas jewelery is worn without function. I think this theory is really silly and don't agree. Many fine artists today have commerciality in mind. On the other hand, many designers (product, jewelry, footwear) make pieces that are experimental and without commerciality in mind. We need artists and designers who want to push ideas further, even if it means somehow losing out commercially.

My "Project" shoes have always been meant as total experiments that I often didn't intend anyone else to see, made purely because I wanted to test something or push an idea to its limits. However, when some journalists and press saw the "Project" shoes, they wanted to feature them, and we ended up getting orders. In this way one could say they are not art, because they were sold, but when I designed them, selling was never the purpose, so therefore they could be regarded as art.

CAT POTTER: My collections have been based on historical objects and cultures. They are also strongly influenced by architecture, furniture design, and organic forms and structures. The notion of transforming a strong and durable material like wood into different forms is something that fascinates me. Transformation is a notion that has always interested me, using dress and form as a way of manipulating identity.

ELIZABETH SEMMELHACK: I first became interested in the cultural meaning of high heels working on an exhibition on the history of Chinese foot-binding. People see lotus shoes for what they are, remarkable and impractical items of dress with complex cultural meanings. The high heel is truly an unusual and counterintuitive addition to a shoe—it does not aid in walking or in comfort—but it has become so naturalized within the female wardrobe that it is almost invisible.

RENÉ VAN DEN BERG/KARIN JANSSEN (A SHOE CAN BE): All our projects start with an image we visualize, inspired by structures of nature, an intriguing object, or special material characteristics.

SEX, HEELS, AND POWER

GABRIEL ASFOUR, ADI GIL, AND ANGELA DONHAUSER (threeASFOUR): Elevation is the key for elegance: high heels make the body look more slim and elongated. Also the arch of the foot is accentuated, giving the foot a more refined contour and silhouette.

BRIAN ATWOOD: I have had plenty of men thank me for my shoes. In fact, a few people credit my sexy shoes with many romantic interludes. There probably is a correlation between my being a male designer and the way I design, which is more over the top and exaggerated. However, I always know that the bottom line comes from how women feel in Brian Atwood.

Men's and women's love of the high heel is simply a reflection of human sexuality. Wearing high heels is a privilege women alone have. Therefore men lust after the gorgeous women in heels. Shoes are in effect a mode of foreplay. It is why the Brian Atwood brand tagline is "The sex is in the heel."

Femininity and feminism should not fight against each other. If people truly believe in empowering women, I believe that we must celebrate all elements that make women feel feminine. This includes, but is not limited to, wearing glamorous shoes.

PIERRE HARDY: People love a high heel because it is not natural. It is a cultural object connected with seduction, power, and sexuality. . . . Power is a question of centimeters. "Size matters," and a woman who is 10 or 12 centimeters taller addresses men differently. The game of "domination" can start. At the opposite end, the pure, evanescent, blurry barefoot nymph is a real fantasy too!

What is sexy? Is it the fragility that the shoes create or, on the contrary, the aggressiveness that they suggest? Or both at the same time? Which fantasy do they create? For myself, I try to give the woman an instrument of self-confidence. I am not sure that women are wearing high heels only for men. There is a true competition on the height of the heel among women! The woman has the choice to turn her high heels into a strength or a

weakness. She can make herself feel more confident or pretend she is vulnerable. I think it is just a game of roles.

REM D. KOOLHAAS (UNITED NUDE): High heels are the only thing in the world that makes a woman taller while completely changing her posture or pose. The change in posture is the most important part, as it straightens the legs and curves the back, bringing out the woman's butt and breasts. This makes a woman look sexier, and this empowers her. This is perhaps not cultural, but purely natural human instinct, and that's the beauty of it all.

MASAYA KUSHINO: Women are gaining stature in the world and high heels give that to them physically. Marilyn Monroe once wore a pair of heels where the heel on one shoe was shorter than the other, which made her walk very unbalanced; her body swayed and that was considered sexy. But heels now are sturdy, strong, and powerful, so the image is changing. Society's preferences are changing. They want strong women.

A woman wore Matthew Barney's crystal shoes after she had her feet amputated. And she is still sexy. This left a strong impression on me. It shows the potential and what's possible with high heels.

ALESSANDRA LANVIN (APERLAÏ): Male and female designers' approaches are different, for sure, but both are part of a complementary vision of the woman. When I created Aperlaï, the idea was to realize a graphic signature of shoes with pure lines, a strong yet feminine design. I also realized that the majority of women's shoe designers are men and thought that creating from a woman's perspective could make a difference.

The reason for women's never-ending love affair with shoes is they have the power of expression. They have the power to instantly transform you, adding those few supplementary inches that glamorize the silhouette and give you a certain allure.

CHRISTIAN LOUBOUTIN: The relationship between high heels and power is extremely subjective. The type of power a woman may feel from a shoe is definitely rooted in her personality and what she wants to derive from it. The high heel by itself doesn't give any power: the heel complements the power the woman already feels she has. . . .

High heels give some women the pleasure of feeling taller and perhaps appearing more fragile. There may be something sweet in this fragility, so sometimes the power is an operation of charm. Some men like a woman to look fragile so they can feel the need to protect her. It's more like a game in a way, and sometimes the power is coming from different directions. I think what heels offer is that they anchor you, in the sense that they fix you to the ground, while at the same time they elevate you. How one responds to that is really unique to each woman. . . .

I think with female designers, the concept of comfort is probably stronger, because they actually try on the shoes, but apart from that I think the essence of design is imagination and it is as strong in women as it is in men. I wouldn't separate designers by their sex, but more by their point of view and their taste for practicality. Some women design completely from their imagination and some are more practical in their approach, just as some men love functionality and some have their heads in the clouds.

JULIA LUNDSTEN (FINSK): A woman will only truly feel powerful if she is in control, and she will only be in control if she is able to move and walk confidently in her heels. I try to design my shoes in such a way that even if they are quite extreme, the last and basic shapes are always good for the wearer's foot, so she can feel confident in moving around. Of course a high heel will never be as comfortable as a flat, cushioned trainer, for example, so it's always a challenge in some ways to wear a high heel. But when you find a high heel that is well designed and you are able to move confidently, it definitely adds power. I think the old-fashioned tendency toward super-high, skinny stilettos and uncomfortable shoes is something certain men like to see women in, but I don't believe these men find the women powerful—quite the contrary.

One of the reasons I first launched FINSK in 2004 was that I simply couldn't find well-designed, cool, high-quality heels for "real women" to wear. Everything was so super-high or had such super-skinny heels that you would only be able to wear them from taxi to taxi. That's why I really focused on modern, wearable midheel designs. Although FINSK is also known for the more outrageous and high "Project" shoes, these midheels have actually always been a staple of each collection since we launched. I do believe it helps to be a modern woman designing for modern, independent women.

WINDE RIENSTRA: I do not want to sexualize the wearer of my high heels; I do not think that way while designing. My designs don't radiate sexiness, although I do think the posture of the models and wearers is sexier for wearing high heels. My high-heel designs are intended to elongate the body, to make a statement, and to contribute to the concept of the collection. I use unexpected and unconventional materials, with which the wearer can make a bold statement. I also think comfort is very important: the heels I design for my collections are very conceptual, but I am looking to produce some more wearable designs based on and inspired by the original conceptual idea. Although I do want the women who wear my heels to feel sexy, I think that it's a totally different sexiness from what men have in mind.

ELIZABETH SEMMELHACK: High heels entered Western fashion first through masculine dress, and for the first 130 years of the fashion, both men and women wore heeled footwear. It was only in the eighteenth century that men abandoned high heels and they became an accessory of female dress associated with irrational yet desirable femininity.

High heels are often posited as accessories of female power, which is typically characterized as "sexual power." But this type of power requires the judgment of others—the value, power, or success of sexual appeal rests in the eye of the beholder. The power lies with those who stand in judgment rather than those who present themselves to be judged. Because high heels are inappropriate on little girls and, for many, seem incongruous on older women, then even if we were to accept that sexual power is a real form of power, then women only have access to it for a relatively short period of their lives.

High heels and platforms have historically conveyed very different meanings. The high heel has been linked with eroticism, while the platform seems to be more closely aligned with play. Although it became a staple in fashion throughout the late 1930s and 1940s, the platform was expressly disliked by men. The privileging of the high heel in men's erotica in the middle of the century further illustrated the divide between the sexy high heel and fashionable platform. This divide repeated itself in the 1970s when platforms became fashionable again, and I think that a bit of a schism remains even today.

HIGH HEELS AND ARCHITECTURE

BRIAN ATWOOD: Even if you have no formal training in architecture, all shoe designers have to be a bit of an architect. High heels are functional structures no different from a suspension bridge or an archway. The way a heel is stacked can literally make or break a shoe. I see heels in many buildings. And like a good architect, a shoe designer has to think about how a heel will be perceived now and in the future. I design a collection thinking about how it will show today and as part of history.

ZAHA HADID: There is the perception of architecture as different from fashion because it is a more immersive experience—it's about how the person places herself in the space—whereas fashion is about how you place the object on the person.

. . . Our experimentation and research into increased complexity in architecture have led us on the path toward natural systems. In shoe design, too, you have to understand how they land, how you can balance, and how you can start walking on them. The striations and realignments of the "Nova" design express the forces applied to the shoes by the wearer and are similar to the natural forms created by dynamic forces within nature.

JULIAN HAKES: At the simplest level, fashion could be described as architecture for the body—with shoes and footwear part of the cladding. Designers wrap, protect, hide, reveal, or enhance parts of the body. My experience in architecture has had a very strong influence and impact on the way I approach design, material and color choice, process of manufacture, packaging, how the shoe looks on the shelf and feels both in the hand and on the foot. With shoes and footwear there are clear structural and dynamic issues to consider, but I feel these are taken as a given by many shoe designers. It was only when I cut open a traditional heel that I realized what an ugly, inefficient mix of rough materials was used to support the foot. This structure is then dressed and decorated to hide it and make it visually pleasing. Designers who don't follow the same narrow format come up with some amazing and liberating creations. Designing through an architectural process and being influenced by architecture are very different—I think the first gives scope for real innovation, creativity, and design, and the latter generates more of a stylistic leaning and is more about decoration of existing shoe typologies.

PIERRE HARDY: Heels are probably, with the corset, the "hardware" of fashion. So in this sense the high heel can be treated, as long as it can still play its anatomical function, as an architectural or sculptural object. But I think there is an enormous difference between design (or architecture) and fashion. Fashion doesn't respond to rational rules or needs. If, as Le Corbusier said, a house is a "machine à habiter" (machine for living), a fashionable shoe is far from the ideal and functional "machine à marcher" (machine for walking), even if some architectural rules regulate the construction and engineering of shoes. Some specialized or sports shoes are functional, but they are not supposed to be fashionable. They can turn into fashion, but as a second life.

REM D. KOOLHAAS (UNITED NUDE): I was trained as an architect, and without a premeditated plan, I was suddenly making shoes. Architecture is big and slow, and shoes are much smaller and faster. Shoes are perhaps the smallest form of a portable architecture: they are structural designs carrying and protecting humans. The launch of our "Möbius" in 2003 introduced a shoe that was designed and made differently from any conventional shoe out there. It was a shoe that didn't look like anything before—a shoe with a new silhouette that was designed as a whole. Sometimes people from outside a field or industry need to come in and stir things up. We ended up breaking the

rules of shoes, not because we wanted to, but simply by not knowing them. But architects scaling down and having an impact on modern daily life was not new. Modernists such as Mies van der Rohe, Le Corbusier, and many others designed furniture for manufacturing nearly a century ago. I'm pretty sure they would have designed shoes if they could, but I guess the materials available then were just not ready for shoes.

CHRISTIAN LOUBOUTIN: High-heel design is very much linked to architecture in terms of center of gravity and weight distribution. My work is definitely influenced by architects who have strong associations with curves, like Oscar Niemeyer and Hassan Fathy, whose arches specifically resonate in the curves and arches of high-heeled shoes. I'm also influenced by the artisans who created the curved legs and feet of the eighteenth-century Louis XV style.

JULIA LUNDSTEN (FINSK): I often think of shoes as "minibuildings" for the feet. There is a lot of engineering and detail similar to that in architecture, so I think it's quite natural that shoe designers look at architecture for inspiration and architects are intrigued by shoes and want to have a go. Shoes have their own architecture and engineering, though, so it's not always as easy without actual experience in designing and producing shoes.

WINDE RIENSTRA: Though I'm not an architect, I am aware that I am influenced by architecture as I work on my designs. Often reviewers have described my collections as "fashion meets architecture." Just because I am not an architect, but feel strongly inspired by it, doesn't mean that I am merely styling shoes or decorating existing shoe typologies. With my first shoe design, however, I started out that way, but after that I always designed and made my heels from scratch. I work differently from traditional shoemakers and shoe-designing architects: I approach my designs less technically and more conceptually. I always choose the material first, and then I shape that in the form and fit. I don't think this makes my shoes

less original, though; as Rem D. Koolhaas says, people from outside a field or industry can successfully break the rules and be innovative.

RENÉ VAN DEN BERG/KARIN JANSSEN (A SHOE CAN BE): A high-heeled shoe is in a way a very small building. There are many similarities in both the development and the final result. Architects and shoe designers search for the perfect balance between construction, material, and appearance. Mixing form, function, and finance, they can create mass products as well as eye-catching icons.

TECHNOLOGY, MATERIALS, AND PROCESS

GABRIEL ASFOUR, ADI GIL, AND ANGELA DONHAUSER (threeASFOUR): Our clothing comes first, and the heel is an extension of the silhouette.

BRIAN ATWOOD: Whether it's an exotic skin or supple leather, the material first speaks to me, dictating my design. My studio is filled with my inspiration sketchbooks, which combine materials, images, and color palettes for reference when I start designing my collections.

The process of translating a design idea into a shoe starts with the sketch. From there, prototypes are made, in order to see how the design looks in 3-D. Usually there are several revisions. Designing high heels is an art, not unlike sculpture. For me, it's all about proportion. Not only when a shoe is standing alone, but also when it's on the foot. Sometimes the negative space occupied by the foot and leg is as important as the heel. The process is further complicated by having to make art that is wearable. Some of my most acclaimed styles were defined by how they looked when in motion. Fringe, feathers, and reflective materials can completely change a shoe when a woman walks.

Technology has brought interesting advances in materials, especially the use of laser techniques. Specifically, lasers allow precision cutout detail that makes an intricate design look effortless and luxe. Also, I have seen a big improvement in bonding techniques, allowing more variation in construction. However, none of these advances replaces the art and craft of hand-finishing shoes, particularly the way it is done in Italy!

ZAHA HADID: One of the most satisfying things about working with United Nude is the technologies used for design and manufacture—the production process between idea and result is so much quicker than for architecture. This faster time frame leads to greater opportunities for experimentation, particularly in the design of an object like a shoe, where we have the possibility to create real prototypes very quickly and we can immediately evaluate the design and comfort.

JULIAN HAKES: I start with the foot and the natural way we need to support the body, and investigate the biomechanics. I considered the footprint in the sand and the way this shows how the body transfers load through walking. As I was not formally trained in footwear, I had no real limitations, so I used the latest materials and techniques available to me, like 3-D printing and the advanced 3-D CAD [computer-aided design] and the parametric software we used for our bridge designs. This allowed us to quickly make a 3-D print of a prototype and test-fit it on a model, study, modify, 3-D scan, and then repeat the process. The materials we selected were all advanced composites more commonly found in aeronautics and sports-car design than footwear.

PIERRE HARDY: Concept and silhouette are definitely for me the most important elements, to start. The concept, if it is a good one, will bring a new way of doing things, a new approach.

A computer can visualize and materialize, even virtually, the product before it's properly made. Because it creates shapes, textures, mixings, almost instantly, it gives us a taste of certain images that were not possible before. It has probably shaped our view as much as classic art.

I would be tempted to say that my designs don't tell a story, because I always try to propose new shapes. But I have to consider that once the collection is finished, it projects some allusion or metaphor that people interpret. So, in the end, it tells a story, but I hope it is a *new* story.

MASAYA KUSHINO: In Japanese we say I have a *hikidashi* (drawers), which is like saying I have a set of drawers filled with ideas. Sometimes I open one drawer and then open another drawer and mix the ideas. This is interesting, as they combine to become an idea I didn't expect. I then decide the material, technique, form, and details, and then I draw. Last, I fix and adjust the balance of the colors or the materials in the design and make minor changes to the details. Then I make a sample, check, and finish.

Some of my shoes represent a short scene and some tell a longer story. For my "Stairway to Heaven" shoes, I imagined the person who wears the shoes walking to heaven on a stairway.

ALESSANDRA LANVIN (APERLAÏ): I like working with natural textures like exotic skins, python, and stingray. My last collections were conceived with the idea of combining nature with new-tech processes and materials like PVC, holographic snakeskin, and laser cutting.

CHAU HAR LEE: I begin with the foot or the last and play around with materials and shapes. I try to ignore the assumptions of what a shoe should look like or how it should be made, although my technical knowledge is important for working out what is possible.

My collections always must involve some conceptual pieces in order for me to realize my idea, which I then take further into more accessible pieces. I often employ manufacturing processes from fields other than shoemaking. This gives me a lot of scope for creativity by removing boundaries associated with traditional methods. However, my knowledge of traditional shoemaking helps me know how and where I can break these rules. Although my most conceptual designs are showpieces, they are still built to adorn the foot.

CHRISTIAN LOUBOUTIN: I don't think I have ever been especially interested in new technologies or new materials. It doesn't matter to me whether a material or technique is new or old; what matters is the way you use it and how it can express one's creativity and vision. . . .

I think that the ultimate high heels have already been invented; the twentieth century is not responsible for inventing these extremes—look at the height of shoes in sixteenth-century Venice, for example.

JULIA LUNDSTEN (FINSK): One of my concepts is to work with traditional, natural materials, such as wood and leather, but use them in a very modern way. The inspiration is based more on architectural and product-design details, so I had to find manufacturers from those fields rather than from footwear to make the heels. I've worked with the same craftsman now for some years, and although I've learned a lot from him and traditional techniques, I've also pushed him to work with the materials in a new and unexpected way.

I start with the silhouette. When building up a collection, the first things to be determined are the shapes, heel heights, and toe shapes. The choice of materials is done at this stage, too. After that come the actual design details. I have set myself some "aesthetic rules" for FINSK shoes, one of them being that there is no actual embellishment or decoration. The detail and design derive from materials and practical solutions, such as a seam that joins together two parts.

I test things, draw up details inspired by furniture or architectural details, and I modify them and work on them. I also experiment with different shapes and colors as prototypes long before the shoe design goes into sampling.

CAT POTTER: I'm fascinated by how 3-D printing is changing footwear architecture and how it can identify new design constructions. At this stage I am still reluctant to use it within my designs, however, as I feel that the material available is very limited. CNC [computer-numerical-controlled] milling has influenced my designs and manufacturing processes for two seasons now. Because of my interest in art and architecture, my designs rely heavily on volumes and silhouettes that can't be achieved through traditional footwear construction. I therefore have to use innovative and cross-disciplinary technologies to create unusual forms.

I very much enjoy working with natural materials like leather or wood. CAD/CAM [computer-aided design and manufacturing] technology and rapid prototyping ordinarily print designs out of nylon, but I wanted to challenge that notion by marrying the technology with a natural material like wood. Its organic appearance and texture contrast starkly with the lines that CNC milling creates.

WINDE RIENSTRA: Being educated as a fashion designer, I had no specific knowledge of footwear. I wanted to finish off my clothing collections with heels that would enhance the overall look, so I approached the heels the same way I do my clothing: first there's the material I want to work in, and ideas develop from experimenting with the materials. After the choice of material comes the fit, and then finding the shape I'm looking for and building my design around that. I love to use unconventional materials, but the most important thing is for the shoes to be a counterbalance in that specific collection.

RENÉ VAN DEN BERG / KARIN JANSSEN (A SHOE CAN BE): A sculpture is always the first step. We develop new materials and explore the tension between form and function, making many preliminary studies. The focus is on balance and a perfect fit.

Curiosity to push limits is an important characteristic of a designer. New techniques and materials must be explored. High heels are the perfect objects for making a statement. And of course, like haute couture, extreme shoes also contribute to new wearable shoe concepts. We treasure craft, incorporating its heritage with new techniques such as 3-D printing. We intend to create unique and personalized products to be cherished a lifetime. We aim to respect our environment, making new materials out of existing ones and not using leather made from animals raised only for their skin.

GABRIEL ASFOUR, ADI GIL, AND ANGELA DONHAUSER (threeASFOUR): Heels are getting higher and higher, with an explosion in recent years of platforms that have allowed heels to get higher still. The technology used to support the foot is developing faster and faster, and thus heels will naturally get higher. The 3-D technology that is slowly taking over the industry allows for structures and materials that were not possible before that enable a less dense and more flexible sole. Materials that can withstand strain and retain more memory will naturally allow the possibility of a higher heel. In twenty years we will be able to levitate. High heels will probably be much more aerodynamic and look more like flying saucers.

BRIAN ATWOOD: Hopefully, we will see many changes in shoes in the next two decades. Obviously, materials will significantly advance. New materials that are eco-sensitive and possibly vegan will develop, for sure. I hope to see science advance LED technology to adapt to fashion. Imagine a shoe made with such technology that it could change color depending on your outfit. I'd even like to see convertible heels, which could adjust in height depending on a woman's mood, outfit, or foot fatigue. Of course making such ideas still glamorous will be the ever-present challenge.

JULIAN HAKES: I think it is interesting to look at footwear in films, especially the more sci-fi high-tech films. Films like *Blade Runner*, *Tron*, and *Star Wars* all have strong fashion and footwear designs. I think that when stylists and filmmakers are looking to the future they are released from the everyday and more liberated to design with new eyes. Change is already here—it's just not all in the public domain yet. There are many people doing 3-D-printed shoes already direct to order, and domestic 3-D printing will have a huge impact on consumers. We will start to consume fashion and design in a way not seen before—probably more like iTunes for your feet. I think we will see this change in five years and even sooner.

PIERRE HARDY: It will depend on the future fantasies we have, and the evolution of technology. All these shapes are just some metaphors of the dreams we have. They don't make us walk better, or faster, or farther. They just make us believe that we could.

MASAYA KUSHINO: In my fantasy, we will go to outer space and there will be no gravity, so we won't need high heels. Shoes will become heelless. If we use high heels, it will only be for style. There will be shoes that have engines or propellers to move through space. Shoes will become vehicles. Shoes and robots will be combined, and shoes will become mobile. It will be a dream. . . . I want to be the first person to make shoes for outer space!

CHRISTIAN LOUBOUTIN: In a creative environment, you cannot speak of what is going to happen in twenty years. Design is influenced by so many different things that evolve and change through time, so it is impossible to say what the distant future might look like. Every year, every day, will make an impression, and you cannot take a short cut to the future.

JULIA LUNDSTEN (FINSK): I think there will be improvement in small hidden components within the shoes, such as better-cushioned insoles or better flexibility and durability, but a high heel is linked to not only technological advances but also imagination, power, and fantasy, among other things. Advances in running shoes, for example, are purely there to increase the performance, whereas high heels are a choice for women, and beauty and style will always play a big role in their design. I do believe ethical and ecological production values and high quality will be the future.

WINDE RIENSTRA: Maybe we will be able to scan our feet at home, upload the image, and decide on the height of the heel, color, material, and shape. There would be a program to pull, shape, and model your shoes; you then order them exactly the way you want them, and they will be 3-D-printed and delivered to your home within a week. They would fit like a glove. In the future I hope we will have developed a lot of new innovative and durable materials that are environmentally friendly. Hopefully, we will only produce shoes that we can upcycle or recycle, or are biodegradable. I hope we can find a way to produce a material that looks and acts like leather, in order to not kill animals for their skin.

PREFACE AND ACKNOWLEDGMENTS

1. For a detailed social history of the high heel, see Elizabeth Semmelhack, *Heights of Fashion: A History of the Elevated Shoe* (Toronto: Bata Shoe Museum Foundation; Pittsburgh, Pa.: Periscope Publishing, 2008); and Elizabeth Semmelhack, *On a Pedestal: From Renaissance Chopines to Baroque Heels* (Toronto: Bata Shoe Museum Foundation and Moveable Inc., 2009).

2. Quoted in Semmelhack, *On a Pedestal*, 74.

3. Quoted in ibid., 72.

4. For coverage of this story, see Megan Garber, "What Does It Mean to Wear Heels?," *Atlantic* online, October 23, 2013, http://www.theatlantic.com/technology/archive/2013/10/what-does-it-mean-to-wear-heels/280810/. See also "Room for Debate: Giving Stilettos the Business," in *New York Times* online, November 1, 2013, http://www.nytimes.com/roomfordebate/2013/11/01/giving-stilettos-the-business.

5. Philip Rucker and Juliet Eilperin, "White House Counsel Kathy Ruemmler: From Outsider to Protector of the Presidency," *Washington Post* online, May 26, 2013, http://www.washingtonpost.com/politics/white-house-counsel-kathy-ruemmler-from-outsider-to-protector-of-the-presidency/2013/05/26/78a6986e-c3f0-11e2-914f-a7aba60512a7_story.html. Amanda Hess reports on the story in "Journalism's Louboutin Problem," in *Slate* online, http://www.slate.com/blogs/xx_factor/2013/05/28/kathryn_ruemmler_wears_shoes_how_journalists_use_louboutins_and_manolo_blahniks.html.

6. "A White House Counsel Known for Her Shoes," by Juliet Eilperin, *Washington Post* online, May 27, 2013, http://www.washingtonpost.com/blogs/the-fix/wp/2013/05/27/a-white-house-counsel-and-her-glamorous-shoes/.

7. "Meditations on Versailles," from *Paris Sketch Book*, in *The Works of William Makepeace Thackeray*, vol. 7 (1840; Boston: James R. Osgood & Company, 1872), 249.

THE ETERNAL HIGH HEEL: EROTICISM AND EMPOWERMENT

1. See Roy C. Flickinger, *The Greek Theater and Its Drama* (Chicago, 1922), 162, Google Books. See also Kendall K. Smith, "The Use of the High-Soled Shoe or Buskin in Greek Tragedy of the Fifth or Fourth Centuries B.C.," *Harvard Studies* 16 (1905), 123ff.; and

Arthur E. Haigh, *The Attic Theatre: A Description of the Stage and Theatre of the Athenians, and of the Dramatic Performances at Athens* (Oxford: Clarendon Press, 1889).

2. Quoted in Millia Davenport, *The Book of Costume*, vol. 1 (New York: Crown, 1948), 196.

3. As Harold Koda has written: "Sixteenth-century accounts suggest that the chopine's height was associated with the level of nobility and grandeur of the Venetian woman who wore them." See Harold Koda, "The Chopine," in *Heilbrunn Timeline of Art History* (New York: Metropolitan Museum of Art, 2000–), http://metmuseum.org.toah/hd/chop/hd_chop.htm.

4. See Elizabeth Semmelhack, *On a Pedestal: From Renaissance Chopines to Baroque Heels* (Toronto: Bata Shoe Museum Foundation and Moveable Inc., 2009); and Anita Singh, "Platform Shoes Were Born in the 16th Century as Symbols of Wealth," *Telegraph* (London), February 24, 2010.

5. William Shakespeare, *Hamlet* (act 2, scene 2), quoted in Jonathan Walford, *The Seductive Shoe: Four Centuries of Fashion Footwear* (New York: Stewart, Tabori & Chang, 2007), 13. The person Hamlet so addresses is one of the Players he has hired to help him "catch the conscience of the king," his fratricidal uncle Claudius, in a performance of *The Mouse-Trap*.

6. See Elizabeth Semmelhack, *Heights of Fashion: A History of the Elevated Shoe* (Toronto: Bata Shoe Museum Foundation; Pittsburgh, Pa: Periscope Publishing, 2008), 74–75.

7. See Hong Jiang, "The Manchu Woman from Head to Toe: An Overview of Qing Dynasty Fashion," in *Epoch Times: English Edition*, November 10, 2011, www.theepochtimes.com/n2/china-news/the-manchu-woman-from-head-to-toe-1; and "Height of Fashion," Peabody Museum of Archaeology and Ethnology at Harvard University website, https://peabody.harvard.edu/node/516.

8. Walford, *The Seductive Shoe*, 13.

9. See Semmelhack, *Heights of Fashion*, 12; and Koda, "The Chopine."

10. Semmelhack, *Heights of Fashion*, 12–14.

11. The *talon rouge* is clearly visible on the royal foot in both Jean Ranc, *Louis XV*, 1718, which depicts Louis XV as an eight-year-old child, and Antoine-François Callet, *Louis XVI in Grand Royal Costume*, 1789, Louis XVI's last official portrait to be completed before the French Revolution toppled his throne (and claimed his head). Both portraits are held by the Musée National des Châteaux de Versailles et de Trianon.

12. See Marie-Josèphe Bossan, *The Art of the Shoe* (London: Parkstone International, 2012), e-book, chap. titled "From Antiquity Up to Our Days."

13. The copyrighted drawings of Napoleon's coronation shoes by Jean-Baptiste Isabey—based on Bonaparte's specifications—were sold by Christie's in 2004 and can be seen at http://www.frenchempirecollection.com/coronation_shoes.html. See also the 1805 coronation portraits by Jacques-Louis David and François Gérard, both of whom clearly depict the heelless white slippers the French emperor wore for the occasion.

14. Semmelhack, *Heights of Fashion*, 36–37.

15. François Boucher, *20,000 Years of Fashion: The History of Costume and Personal Adornment* (New York: Harry N. Abrams, 1987), 401, 413.

16. Sigmund Freud, "Fetishism" (1927), in *The Standard Edition of The Complete Psychological Works of Sigmund Freud*, ed. and trans. James Strachey, vol. 21 (London: Hogarth Press, 1961), 147–57.

17. Ibid., 153. "The foot or shoe," Freud explains, "owes its preference as a fetish . . . to the circumstance that the inquisitive boy peered at the woman's genitals from below, from her legs up" (155).

18. Semmelhack, *Heights of Fashion*, 42–43.

19. Quoted in ibid., 42.

20. Sarah Churchwell, *The Many Lives of Marilyn Monroe* (New York: Picador, 2005), 55.

REVIVAL AND REINTERPRETATION

1. "The Philosophy of Dress," *New-York Tribune*, Apr. 19, 1885, 9.

2. "Salvatore Ferragamo: Shoes" (1973.282.6), in *Heilbrunn Timeline of Art History* (New York: Metropolitan Museum of Art, 2000–), http://www.metmuseum.org/toah/works-of-art/1973.282.6 (October 2006).

3. The sculpture, *Marilyn AP* (2011), is meant as a commentary on women's achievements in the private and public spheres.

4. Wigs depicting naval battles were the fashionable way that many French aristocratic women demonstrated their patriotism in 1778, when France's navy fought with the United States against England. Although Marie Antoinette was famous for her elaborate wigs, there is no evidence that she herself actually wore one with a ship.

5. See Elizabeth Semmelhack, *Heights of Fashion: A History of the Elevated Shoe* (Toronto: Bata Shoe Museum Foundation; Pittsburgh, Pa.: Periscope Publishing, 2008), 40–44. I have relied on this book, as well as Elizabeth Semmelhack, *On a Pedestal: From Renaissance Chopines to Baroque Heels* (Toronto: Bata Shoe Museum Foundation and Moveable Inc., 2009), for much of the historical information in the section texts.

6. Ibid, 55.

RISING IN THE EAST

1. For detailed information about the Eastern origins of the platform shoe, see Elizabeth Semmelhack, *On a Pedestal: From Renaissance Chopines to Baroque Heels* (Toronto: Beta Shoe Museum Foundation and Moveable Inc., 2009).

2. See Martha Chaiklin, "Purity, Pollution and Place in Traditional Japanese Footwear," in *Shoes: A History from Sandals to Sneakers*, ed. Giorgio Riello and Peter McNeil, 160–81 (Oxford: Berg, 2006).

3. See Elizabeth Semmelhack, *Roger Vivier: Process to Perfection* (Toronto: Bata Shoe Museum Foundation, 2012), 39.

GLAMOUR AND FETISH

1. Among the films depicting stiletto violence are *Butterfield 8* (1960), in which Elizabeth Taylor grinds her heel into Laurence Harvey's foot, and *Single White Female* (1992), where a man is killed with a stiletto. Life imitates art: a woman in Texas was recently charged with murder for striking a man "with a deadly weapon, namely a shoe." "Professor Killed by Woman with Stiletto Heel, Police Say," by Josh Levs, CNN online, June 12, 2013. http://www.cnn.com/2013/06/11/justice/texas-stiletto-stabbing/.

2. Louboutin's shoes and Lynch's photographs were shown in 2007 at an exhibition called *Fetish* at the Galerie du Passage in Paris. See Christian Louboutin, Eric Reinhart, Philippe Garcia, David Lynch, and John Malkovich, *Christian Louboutin* (New York: Rizzoli, 2011), 239–59.

ARCHITECTURE

1. Roger Vivier and Salvatore Ferragamo are most often credited as "inventing" the steel-reinforced stiletto, although André Perugia made an early version of it in 1951, Many designers were simultaneously working on the idea of a high, thin heel, which was much in demand, and there may be no way to establish who was first. See Elizabeth Semmelhack, *Roger Vivier: Process to Perfection* (Toronto: Beta Shoe Museum Foundation, 2012).

METAMORPHOSIS

1. Charles Perrault's 1697 version described the central magical shoe as a *pantoufle de verre,* or glass slipper. (Whether the word *vair,* meaning "fur," was mistranslated as "glass" is still debated.) He made no reference to the height of the slipper's heel, and most illustrations of the story depict a shoe that conforms to our current notions of what a "slipper" is, having only a modest heel, or no heel at all. Yet by the end of the seventeenth century in Europe, many fashionable aristocratic shoes, including *pantoufles,* or mules, had high heels. As a member of Versailles society, Perrault is likely to have seen this type of shoe peeping from beneath ladies' gowns at the court of King Louis XIV, himself a great proponent of high heels (see Fig. 6).

2. Recent studies have been undertaken to demonstrate that the gait and posture of women walking in high heels are perceived as significantly more attractive than in flat shoes. See Paul H. Morris et al., "High Heels as Supernormal Stimuli: How Wearing High Heels Affects Judgements of Female Attractiveness," *Evolution & Human Behavior* 34, no. 3 (May 2013): 176–81.

3. Elmer Ruan Coates, "The Grecian Bend," musical score (New York: Wm. A. Pond, 1868). In the 1860s fashionable skirts were gathered at the back and piled high on a bustle. Worn with corsets and high heels, the style forced many women to appear to lean forward in an exaggeratedly stooped posture. The Grecian Bend was the nickname given to this distinctive silhouette, which was thought to be reminiscent of the way women in ancient Greek art hunched their shoulders in modesty.

4. Quoted in Marc Linder and Charles L. Saltzman, "A History of Medical Scientists on High Heels," *International Journal of Health Services* 28, no. 2 (1998): 201–25.

SPACE WALK

1. The amputee athlete Aimee Mullins famously wore crystal prosthetic legs with integrated high heels in Matthew Barney's film *Cremaster 3* (2003). More recently, a woman who lost her leg in the 2013 Boston Marathon bombing received a prosthetic leg with a foot made to fit in her favorite 4-inch high heels. See http://bigstory.ap.org/article /marathon-bomb-victim-gets-new -leg-high-heels.

Benstock, Shari, and Suzanne Ferriss, eds. *Footnotes: On Shoes.* New Brunswick, N.J.: Rutgers University Press, 2001.

Bossan, Marie-Josèphe. *The Art of the Shoe.* New York: Parkstone International, 2012. E-book.

The Costume Institute. *100 Shoes.* New York: Metropolitan Museum of Art, 2011.

Cox, Caroline. *Stiletto.* New York: Harper Design, 2004.

Ko, Dorothy. *Cinderella's Sisters: A Revisionist History of Footbinding.* Berkeley: University of California Press, 2005.

Koda, Harold. *Extreme Beauty: The Body Transformed.* New York: Metropolitan Museum of Art, 2001.

McDowell, Colin. *Shoes: Fashion and Fantasy.* New York: Rizzoli, 1989.

Mears, Patricia. *Fancy Feet: A Historic Collection of Ladies' Footwear from the Brooklyn Museum.* Tokyo: Fashion Foundation, 1994.

Pratt, Lucy, and Linda Woolley. *Shoes.* London: V&A Publications, 2008.

Reeder, Jan Glier. *High Style: Master- works from the Brooklyn Museum Costume Collection at The Metropolitan Museum of Art.* New York: Metropolitan Museum of Art, 2010.

Riello, Giorgio, and Peter McNeil, eds. *Shoes: A History from Sandals to Sneakers.* Oxford: Berg, 2006.

Semmelhack, Elizabeth. *Fetish: Fashion, Sex & Power.* New York: Oxford University Press, 1996.

———. *Heights of Fashion: A History of the Elevated Shoe.* Toronto: Bata Shoe Museum Foundation; Pittsburgh, Pa.: Periscope Publishing, 2008.

———. *Icons of Elegance: The Most Influential Shoe Designers of the 20th Century.* Toronto: Bata Shoe Museum Foundation, 2005.

———. *On a Pedestal: From Renaissance Chopines to Baroque Heels.* Toronto: Bata Shoe Museum Foundation and Moveable Inc., 2009.

———. *Roger Vivier: Process to Perfection.* Toronto: Bata Shoe Museum Foundation, 2012.

———. *Shoes: A Lexicon of Style.* New York: Rizzoli, 1999.

Steele, Valerie, and Colleen Hill. *Shoe Obsession.* New Haven, Conn.: Yale University Press; New York: Fashion Institute of Technology, 2012.

Trasko, Mary. *Heavenly Soles: Extraordinary Twentieth-Century Shoes.* New York: Abbeville Press, 1989.

Vartanian, Ivan, ed. *High Heels: Fashion, Femininity, Seduction.* New York: Goliga, 2011.

Walford, Jonathan. *The Seductive Shoe: Four Centuries of Fashion Footwear.* New York: Stewart, Tabori & Chang, 2007.

Walker, Harriet. *Cult Shoes: Classic and Contemporary Designers.* London: Merrell, 2012.

Wright, Lee. "Objectifying Gender: The Stiletto Heel." In *A View from the Interior: Feminism, Women and Design,* edited by Judy Attfield and Pat Kirkham, 7–19. London: Women's Press, 1989.

CATALOGUE CHECKLIST

Captions followed by * indicate works not included in the Brooklyn Museum presentation.

1. Manolo Blahnik. "Borli," Spring/Summer 2014. Courtesy of Manolo Blahnik

2. Bernard Figueroa. Mules, circa 1994. Leather, synthetic. Brooklyn Museum Costume Collection at The Metropolitan Museum of Art, Gift of the Brooklyn Museum, 2009; Gift of Bernard Figueroa, 1996. 2009.300.3911a, b

3. Salvatore Ferragamo (Italian, 1898–1960). Shoe, 1948–50. Leather. The Metropolitan Museum of Art, New York, Gift of Salvatore Ferragamo, 1973 (1973.282.6)

4. Italian. Chopines, 1550–1650. Silk, metal. Brooklyn Museum Costume Collection at The Metropolitan Museum of Art, Gift of the Brooklyn Museum, 2009; Gift of Herman Delman, 1955. 2009.300.1494a, b

5. J. Ferry, Paris. Evening Slippers, 1885–90. Silk. Brooklyn Museum Costume Collection at The Metropolitan Museum of Art, Gift of the Brooklyn Museum, 2009; Gift of Mrs. Frederick H. Prince, Jr., 1967. 2009.300.1579a, b

6. Samo (Italian). Pumps, circa 1968. Silk, metal, glass. Brooklyn Museum Costume Collection at The Metropolitan Museum of Art, Gift of the Brooklyn Museum, 2009; Gift of Mrs. Dasha Epstein in memory of her mother, Mimi Leviton Amsterdam, 1978. 2009.300.3366a, b

7. Manolo Blahnik. Evening Shoes, 1990–92. Silk, leather, rhinestones. Brooklyn Museum Costume Collection at The Metropolitan Museum of Art, Gift of the Brooklyn Museum, 2009; Gift of Manolo Blahnik, 1992. 2009.300.1630a, b

8. Roger Vivier. "Rose N' Roll," Fall 2012. Purple satin. Courtesy of Roger Vivier, Paris

9. Delman (American). Evening Shoe, 1935–40. Silk, rhinestones. Brooklyn Museum Costume Collection at The Metropolitan Museum of Art, Gift of the Brooklyn Museum, 2009; Gift of Herman Delman, 1955. 2009.300.1492

10. Salvatore Ferragamo (Italian, 1898–1960). Platform Sandal, 1938. Leather, cork. The Metropolitan Museum of Art, New York, Gift of Salvatore Ferragamo, 1973 (1973.282.2)

11. Casuccio e Scalera per Loris Azzaro (Italian). Sandal, 1974–79. Leather, synthetic material, cotton. The Bata Shoe Museum, P03.0040.AB

12. Brian Atwood. "Paulina," Spring/Summer 2013. Courtesy of Brian Atwood

13. Mary Poppins (Italian). Platform Shoes, circa 1973. Leather. Brooklyn Museum Costume Collection at The Metropolitan Museum of Art, Gift of the Brooklyn Museum, 2009; Gift of Sheri Sandler, 1993. 2009.300.3392a, b

14. Maison Martin Margiela. Boot, Artisanal Autumn/Winter 2013. High boots and wood platforms wrapped in caramel leather with Swarovski crystal cuff. Courtesy of Maison Martin Margiela

15. Pierre Hardy. Platform, Spring 2013. Courtesy of Pierre Hardy

16. Christian Louboutin. "Clovis," Spring/Summer 1996. Patent leather, Plexiglas, hydrangea petals. Courtesy of Christian Louboutin

17. Christian Louboutin. "Marie-Antoinette," Fall/Winter 2008-9. Satin crepe with Lesage embroidery. Courtesy of Christian Louboutin

18. French. Shoes, 1690–1700. Silk, leather. The Metropolitan Museum of Art, New York, Rogers Fund, 1906 (06.1344a, b)

19. André Perugia (French, 1893–1977). Evening Sandals, 1928–29. Leather, metal. Brooklyn Museum Costume Collection at The Metropolitan Museum of Art, Gift of the Brooklyn Museum, 2009; Gift of Mrs. Carleton Putnam, 1981. 2009.300.1612a, b

20. Miu Miu. "Cammeo Baroque" Leather Wedge, Fall/Winter 2006. Courtesy of Prada USA Corp.

21. Charles Strohbeck, Inc. (American). Evening Shoes, circa 1920. Cotton, silk. Brooklyn Museum Costume Collection at The Metropolitan Museum of Art, Gift of the Brooklyn Museum, 2009; Gift of Charles Strohbeck, 1964. 2009.300.3265a, b

22. Miu Miu. "Ortensia and Oro" T-strap Pump, Fall/Winter 2013. Courtesy of Prada USA Corp.

23. Enzo Albanese (Italian). Shoes, 1954–58. Leather. Brooklyn Museum Costume Collection at The Metropolitan Museum of Art, Gift of the Brooklyn Museum, 2009; Gift of Charline Osgood, 1960. 2009.300.1531

24. Italian. Shoe, 1700–1730. Velvet, cotton(?), ribbon, leather, metallic thread braid, wood. The Bata Shoe Museum, P87.0185.AB*

25. Pietro Yantorny (Italian, 1874–1936). Pumps, 1925–30. Silk, rhinestones. Brooklyn Museum Costume Collection at The Metropolitan Museum of Art, Gift of the Brooklyn Museum, 2009; Gift of Mrs. Edward G. Sparrow, 1969. 2009.300.1593a, b

26. Salvatore Ferragamo (Italian, 1898–1960). "Booty" Cocktail Boots, 1947. Leather, cotton. Brooklyn Museum Costume Collection at The Metropolitan Museum of Art, Gift of the Brooklyn Museum, 2009; Gift of the Italian Government, 1954. 2009.300.1184a, b

27. Chanel. Heel, Haute Couture, Spring/Summer 2010. Leather, resin, plastic, metal. Courtesy of Chanel

28. John Fluevog. "Munster" Platform Shoes, 1994. Leather, metal. The Metropolitan Museum of Art, New York, Gift of Richard Martin, 1994 (1994.578.1a, b)

29. Delman (American), Bergdorf Goodman (American). Pumps, 1937–39. Leather. Brooklyn Museum Costume Collection at The Metropolitan Museum of Art, Gift of the Brooklyn Museum, 2009; Gift of Mrs. Lewis Iselin Jr., 1960. 2009.300.3784a, b

30. Vivienne Westwood. "Portrait" Shoes, 1990. Leather. The Metropolitan Museum of Art, New York, Millia Davenport and Zipporah Fleisher Fund, 2006 (2006.14a, b)

31. Charles Strohbeck, Inc. (American). Oxford, 1900–1910. Leather. Brooklyn Museum Costume Collection at The Metropolitan Museum of Art, Gift of the Brooklyn Museum, 2009; Gift of Charles Strohbeck, 1964. 2009.300.3842

32. Christian Louboutin. "Super Sling Tassel," Spring/Summer 2006. Satin and tassel. Courtesy of Christian Louboutin

33. Japanese. Sandals, 1984. Wood (kiri), velvet, tatami, lacquer. The Bata Shoe Museum, P84.0073.AB

34. Syrian. Pair of Sandals, 1875–1900. Wood, mother-of-pearl, silver, metal alloy. The Bata Shoe Museum, P11.0005.AB*

35. Italian. Chopines, circa 1600. Leather, wood. The Metropolitan Museum of Art, New York, Purchase, Irene Lewisohn Bequest, 1973 (1973.114.4a, b)

36. Christian Siriano. Pumps, Fall 2013. Courtesy of Christian Siriano

37. Jean Paul Gaultier. "2-in-1 Wedges," Ready-to-Wear Fall/Winter 2010–11. Leather, satin. Courtesy of Maison Jean Paul Gaultier

38. Chinese. Manchu Woman's Shoes, probably late 19th century. Wood, cotton, embroidered satin-weave silk. Brooklyn Museum, Brooklyn Museum Collection, 34.1057a, b

39. Roger Vivier. "Rendez Vous, Limited Edition Blue Feather Choc," Fall/Winter 2013–14. Leather with kingfisher, peacock, goose feathers. Courtesy of Roger Vivier, Paris

40. Rodarte (Kate and Laura Mulleavy). "Ming Printed Leather and Carved Wood Heel," 2011. Courtesy of Rodarte

41. Pietro Yantorny (Italian, 1874–1936). Mules, 1914–19. Silk, metal. Brooklyn Museum Costume Collection at The Metropolitan Museum of Art, Gift of the Brooklyn Museum, 2009; Gift of Mercedes de Acosta, 1953. 2009.300.1459a, b

42. Christian Dior (French, 1905–1957). Roger Vivier (French, 1913–1998) for House of Dior. Evening Slippers, 1960. Silk, metal, synthetic, glass. The Metropolitan Museum of Art, New York, Gift of Valerian Stux-Rybar, 1980 (1980.597.6a, b)

43. Turkish (for Western market). Evening Slippers, 1865–85. Silk, metal. Brooklyn Museum, Gift of Mrs. Clarence R. Hyde, 28.102.10a, b

44. André Perugia (French, 1893–1977) for Paul Poiret (French, 1879–1944). "Le Bal" Slippers, 1924. Silk, glass, leather. The Metropolitan Museum of Art, New York, Purchase, Friends of The Costume Institute Gifts, 2005 (2005.192a, b)

45. Chinese. Manchu Woman's Shoes, probably late 19th century. Cotton, embroidered satin-weave silk. Brooklyn Museum, Brooklyn Museum Collection, 34.1060a, b

46. Prada. Fuoco Silk and Lizard Platform, Spring/Summer 2013. Courtesy of Prada USA Corp.

47. Japanese. Geta, first half of 20th century. Wood, silk, velvet. Brooklyn Museum, Gift of Susan Bass, 76.22.2a, b

48. Martin Margiela, Maison Martin Margiela. Pumps, 2001. Leather. The Metropolitan Museum of Art, New York, Purchase, Judith and Gerson Leiber Fund, 2010 (2010.137a, b)

49. Walter Steiger. "Ishi Wedge," Spring 2011. Courtesy of Walter Steiger

50. Winde Rienstra. "Bamboo Heels," 2012. Bamboo, glue, plastic cable ties. Courtesy of Winde Rienstra

51. Vivienne Westwood. "Rocking Horse Ballerina," 2013 (original design 1985). Leather, wood. Courtesy of Vivienne Westwood

52. Beth Levine (American, 1914–2006), Herbert Levine Inc. (American). "Kabuki" Mule, circa 1966. Leather, wood. Brooklyn Museum Costume Collection at The Metropolitan Museum of Art, Gift of the Brooklyn Museum, 2009; Gift of Beth Levine in memory of her husband, Herbert, 1994. 2009.300.3393

53. Beth Levine (American, 1914–2006), Herbert Levine Inc. (American). "Kabuki" Evening Shoe, circa 1965. Silk, metal, wood. Brooklyn Museum Costume Collection at The Metropolitan Museum of Art, Gift of the Brooklyn Museum, 2009; Gift of Beth Levine in memory of her husband, Herbert, 1994. 2009.300.1636

54. Jean Paul Gaultier. "Nude Tattoo Boots," Ready-to-Wear Spring/Summer 2012. Leather, plastic, metal. Courtesy of Maison Jean Paul Gaultier

55. Noritaka Tatehana. "Atom," 2012–13. Faux leather. Courtesy of Noritaka Tatehana

56. Christian Louboutin for Manish Malhotra. Platform, 2013. Courtesy of Christian Louboutin

57. Giuseppe Zanotti. Heels, Fall/Winter 2012–13. Courtesy of Giuseppe Zanotti

58. Salvatore Ferragamo (Italian, 1898–1960). Marilyn Monroe's Salvatore Ferragamo Pump, 1959. Black calf. Museo Salvatore Ferragamo, Florence

59. Richard Braqo. "Benedetta," 2012. Suede, metal heel, plastic sole. Courtesy of Richard Braqo

60. Dal Co' (Italian). Pumps, 1956. Leather, metal. Brooklyn Museum Costume Collection at The Metropolitan Museum of Art, Gift of the Brooklyn Museum, 2009; Gift of Charline Osgood, 1960. 2009.300.1268a, b

61. Giuseppe Zanotti. Heel, Spring/Summer 2014. Courtesy of Giuseppe Zanotti

62. United Nude. "Gaga Shoe," 2012. Leather, metal. Courtesy of United Nude

63. Nicholas Kirkwood. Pumps, Spring/Summer 2013. Suede with gold and clear Swarovski crystals. Courtesy of Nicholas Kirkwood

64. Iris van Herpen X United Nude. "Fang," 2012. Courtesy of United Nude

65. Christian Louboutin. "Lipspikes Bootie," Fall/Winter 2010–11. Lambskin, metal. Courtesy of Christian Louboutin. Photo © Christian Louboutin

66. Jean Paul Gaultier. "Mille-Pattes Stilettos," Ready-to-Wear Spring/ Summer 1993. Leather. Courtesy of Maison Jean Paul Gaultier

67. Iris van Herpen X United Nude. "Thorn," 2012. Courtesy of United Nude

68. American. Marabou Mules, 1950–59. Synthetic, feathers. Brooklyn Museum Costume Collection at The Metropolitan Museum of Art, Gift of the Brooklyn Museum, 2009; Gift of Joan Fontaine, 1962. 2009.300.1537a, b

69. Viktor & Rolf. Heel, Spring/Summer 2011. Courtesy of Viktor & Rolf

70. Nicholas Kirkwood. Pumps, Spring/Summer 2013. Black suede and dark gold frill. Courtesy of Nicholas Kirkwood

71. Viktor & Rolf. Mule, Spring/Summer 2012. Courtesy of Viktor & Rolf

72. Brian Atwood. "Sigrid," Spring/Summer 2013. Courtesy of Brian Atwood

73. Charlotte Olympia. "Mae West," Pre-Fall 2013. Satin with embroidery. Courtesy of Charlotte Olympia

74. Alexander McQueen. Lace-up Peep Toe Boots, Spring/Summer 2013. Patent leather and Swarovski crystals. Courtesy of Alexander McQueen. Photo by Chris Moore/Catwalking, © catwalking.com

75. Beth Levine (American, 1914–2006), Herbert Levine Inc. (American). Stocking Shoes, 1953. Silk, synthetic. Brooklyn Museum Costume Collection at The Metropolitan Museum of Art, Gift of the Brooklyn Museum, 2009; Gift of Beth Levine in memory of her husband, Herbert, 1994. 2009.300.2240a, b

76. Aoi Kotsuhiroi. "Forbidden Color," 2013. Cherrywood, horn (heels), black and cinnabar Urushi (tree sap) lacquer, animal glues, vegetable-tanned kangaroo leather (straps). Courtesy of Aoi Kotsuhiroi

77. Maniatis Bottier, Paris. Boots, 1920s. Leather, cellulose. The Metropolitan Museum of Art, New York, Alfred Z. Solomon-Janet A. Sloane Endowment Fund, 2007 (2007.57a, b)

78. Christian Louboutin. "Metropolis," Fall/Winter 2010–11. Calfskin and silver spikes. Courtesy of Christian Louboutin

79. Christian Louboutin. "Big Lips Boots," Fall/Winter 2010–11. Lambskin and metal. Courtesy of Christian Louboutin

80. Christian Louboutin. Pumps, 2007. Leather. The Metropolitan Museum of Art, New York, Gift of Christian Louboutin, 2012 (2012.121a, b)

81. Bray Bros. (American). Evening Boots, circa 1918. Leather. Brooklyn Museum Costume Collection at The Metropolitan Museum of Art, Gift of the Brooklyn Museum, 2009; Gift of Mrs. Roderick Tower, 1961. 2009.300.1536a–d

82. Bernhard Gronberg (Swedish). Shoes, 1923–29. Leather, kid, suede, cotton. The Bata Shoe Museum, P89.0016.AB

83. Dolce & Gabbana. Sandals, Spring/Summer 2003. Leather, metal. The Metropolitan Museum of Art, New York, Gift of Dolce & Gabbana, 2003. (2003.355.2a, b)

84. Christian Louboutin. "Printz," Spring/Summer 2013. Courtesy of Christian Louboutin

85. Vivienne Westwood. "Super Elevated Gillies," 1993. Courtesy of Vivienne Westwood

86. Susan Bennis/Warren Edwards. Pumps, circa 1985. Leather. Brooklyn Museum Costume Collection at The Metropolitan Museum of Art, Gift of the Brooklyn Museum, 2009; Gift of Candice Gold, 1993. 2009.300.1631a, b

87. Georgina Goodman. "LOVE," Spring/Summer 2011. Suede, leather, crystal. Courtesy of Georgina Goodman

88. Jean Paul Gaultier. "Eiffel Tower Pump," Fall/Winter 2000–2001. Metal, fabric, fur. Courtesy of Maison Jean Paul Gaultier

89. Miu Miu. "Nero" Lace-up Platform Heel, Spring/Summer 2008. Courtesy of Prada USA Corp.

90. Enzo Albanese (Italian). Sandal, circa 1958. Leather, metal. Brooklyn Museum Costume Collection at The Metropolitan Museum of Art, Gift of the Brooklyn Museum, 2009; Gift of Margaret Jerrold Inc., 1965. 2009.300.1553

91. European. Pattens, 18th century. Leather, metal. Brooklyn Museum Costume Collection at The Metropolitan Museum of Art, Gift of the Brooklyn Museum, 2009; Gift of Herman Delman, 1954. 2009.300.1485a, b

92. British. Shoes, 1720. Leather, silk, wood, kid. The Bata Shoe Museum, P82.0017.AB*

93. Skyscrapers (American). Stilettos, 1955–57. Leather, textile. The Bata Shoe Museum, S82.0074.AB

94. Roger Vivier. "Virgule Houndstooth," Fall 2014. Calf hair. Courtesy of Roger Vivier, Paris

95. Pierre Hardy. "Skyline Heel," Summer 2011. Courtesy of Pierre Hardy

96. Roger Vivier (French, 1913–1998) for House of Dior. Evening Shoes, 1960. Silk. The Metropolitan Museum of Art, New York, Gift of Valerian Stux-Rybar, 1979 (1979.472.24a, b)

97. Maison Martin Margiela. "Suspended Demi-Pointe Heel," Spring/Summer 2014. Courtesy of Maison Martin Margiela

98. Tea Petrovic. "Wings/Variation," 2013. Polyamide, faux leather, rubber. Courtesy of Tea Petrovic

99. Zaha Hadid X United Nude. "NOVA," 2013. Chromed vinyl rubber, kid napa leather, fiberglass. Courtesy of United Nude

100. Julian Hakes. "Mojito," 2012. Courtesy of Julian Hakes

101. Fendi. Heel, 2013. Leather. Courtesy of Fendi

102. Aperlaï. "Geisha Lines," Fall 2013. Leather. Courtesy of Aperlaï

103. Miu Miu. "Smeraldo" Leather Pumps, Fall/Winter 2008. Courtesy of Prada USA Corp.

104. Christian Dior. Heels, Fall 2013. Courtesy of Christian Dior

105. Winde Rienstra. "Shutter Heels," 2013. Laser-cut Perspex (or Plexiglas), screws, elastic with wood beads. Courtesy of Winde Rienstra

106. Marc Jacobs. Pumps, Spring/Summer 2008. Leather. The Metropolitan Museum of Art, New York, Purchase, Ditty Peto Inc. Gift, 2008 (2008.154a, b)

107. Rem D. Koolhaas. "Eamz," 2004. Courtesy of United Nude

108. Delman (American). Shoes, 1938–40. Leather, wood, kid, silk, textile, paint. The Bata Shoe Museum, P96.0150.AB

109. Victor (American). Platform Sandals, circa 1940. Leather. Brooklyn Museum Costume Collection at The Metropolitan Museum of Art, Gift of the Brooklyn Museum, 2009; Gift of Vivian Mook Baer in memory of Sylvia Terner Mook, 1983. 2009.300.1614a, b

110. Balenciaga by Nicolas Ghesquière. Shoes, Fall/Winter 2010. Produced by Balenciaga, Paris. Leather, wood, metal, foam, various plastics. The Montreal Museum of Fine Arts, promised gift of Balenciaga. Photo: MMFA, Jean-François Brière

111. Rem D. Koolhaas. "Möbius," 2003. Courtesy of United Nude

112. Atalanta Weller. "The Big Shoes," 2008. Poplar wood, matt/gloss paint. Courtesy of Atalanta Weller

113. Cat Potter. "Pernilla, Look 5," 2012. Wood. Courtesy of Cat Potter

114. Projections. Shoes, 1972–76. Leather, suede, rubber. The Bata Shoe Museum, S82.0345.AB

115. Balenciaga. Block Heel, Spring 2013. Courtesy of Marie-Amélie Sauvé

116. Maison Martin Margiela. "Glass Slippers," Spring/Summer 2009. Courtesy of Maison Martin Margiela

117. A SHOE CAN BE (René van den Berg, Karin Janssen). "Heliotrope," 2013. Leather, suede, wood veneer, Swarovski crystals. Courtesy of René van den Berg and Karin Janssen

118. Elsa Schiaparelli (Italian, 1890–1973). Shoe Hat, Winter 1937–38. French. Wool. The Metropolitan Museum of Art, New York, Gift of Rose Messing, 1974 (1974.139)

119. Christian Louboutin. "Déjà vu," Fall/Winter 2011–12. Patent leather, suede, ornamental eyes. Courtesy of Christian Louboutin

120. Céline. "Trompe L'oeil Pump," 2013. Courtesy of Céline

121. Chinese. Shoes for Women's Bound Feet, 19th century. Embroidered satin, wood, paper. Brooklyn Museum Collection, 37.371.104.1, .2

122. Aperlaï. "Pico Hands," Fall/Winter 2013–14. Leather. Courtesy of Aperlaï

123. Helmut Lang. Shoes, Spring/Summer 2003. Synthetic, leather. The Metropolitan Museum of Art, New York, Gift of the artist, 2009 (2009.516.36a, b)

124. Iris van Herpen X United Nude. "Beyond Wilderness," 2013. Courtesy of United Nude

125. Beth Levine (American, 1914–2006), Herbert Levine Inc. (American). Slingback Shoe, circa 1962. Leather. Brooklyn Museum Costume Collection at The Metropolitan Museum of Art, Gift of the Brooklyn Museum, 2009; Gift of Beth Levine in memory of her husband, Herbert, 1994. 2009.300.3907

126. Miu Miu. "Ortensia and Oro" Platform Lace-up Heel, Spring/Summer 2008. Courtesy of Prada USA Corp.

127. Céline. "Fur Pump," Spring 2013. Mink fur. Courtesy of Céline

128. Shoise (Matilda Maroti and Petra Högström). "Mother of Pearl," 2013. Courtesy of Shoise

129. Kerrie Luft. "Thandie," 2013. Teal blue suede with black patent piping, gold titanium heel, black lacquered flower. Courtesy of Kerrie Luft

130. Prada. Sandal in Cipria and Cordovan Leather, Spring/Summer 2008. Courtesy of Prada USA Corp.

131. Iris Schieferstein. "Horse Shoes 3," 2006. Horse fur, horse hoof, wood, zipper. Courtesy of Iris Schieferstein and Frosch & Poortman

132. Maison Martin Margiela. Boot, Spring/Summer 2012. Courtesy of Maison Martin Margiela

133. Masaya Kushino. "Stairway to Heaven," 2013. Goatskin, baby lamb, crow feather. Courtesy of Masaya Kushino

134. Yves Saint Laurent (French, 1936–2008). Yves Saint Laurent Rive Gauche. Shoe, 2004. Feathers, leather, synthetic. The Metropolitan Museum of Art, New York, Gift of Yves Saint Laurent, 2005 (2005.325.2)

135. Tom Ford. Wedge Shoes, Spring 2013. Leather. Courtesy of Tom Ford

136. Isabel Canovas. Pumps, Fall/Winter 1988–89. Silk, metal. The Metropolitan Museum of Art, New York, Gift of Richard Martin, 1993 (1993.34a, b)

137. House of Dior for Delman. Designed by Roger Vivier (French, 1913–1998). Evening Shoe, 1954. Silk, feathers. The Metropolitan Museum of Art, New York, Gift of Valerian Stux-Rybar, 1980 (1980.597.16)

138. Steven Arpad (French, 1904–1999). "Model No. 256" Shoe Prototype, 1939. Leather, wood. Brooklyn Museum Costume Collection at The Metropolitan Museum of Art, Gift of the Brooklyn Museum, 2009; Gift of Arpad 1947, 1947. 2009.300.1127

139. Walter Steiger. "Unicorn Tayss," Spring 2013. Courtesy of Walter Steiger

140. Fendi. Bootie, 2013. Calf hair, mink fur, mirrored heel, leather. Courtesy of Fendi

141. Masaya Kushino. "Chimera," 2011. Cattle hide, fox tail, brass. Courtesy of Masaya Kushino

142. Christian Louboutin. "Puck," Fall/Winter 2011–12. Goatskin and leather. Courtesy of Christian Louboutin

143. JANTAMINIAU. "Tarnished Beauty," 2012. (Handcrafted by René van den Berg.) Courtesy of JANTAMINIAU

144. Rem D. Koolhaas. "Flat Pack Shoe (for Moon Life Project)," 2010. CNC-Eb Prototype. Courtesy of United Nude. © United Nude

145. Givenchy by Riccardo Tisci. Heel, Women's Ready-to-Wear Spring/Summer 2013. Leather, PVC, wood. Courtesy of Givenchy, Paris

146. Andreia Chaves. Invisible "Naked Version," 2011, Invisible Shoe Series. Leather, 3-D-printed nylon. Courtesy of Andreia Chaves. © Andreia Chaves. Photo: Andrew Bradley

147. Chau Har Lee. "Blade Heel," 2010. Perspex, stainless steel, leather. Courtesy of Chau Har Lee

148. Salvatore Ferragamo (Italian, 1898–1960). "Invisible" Sandals, 1947. Leather, synthetic. Brooklyn Museum Costume Collection at The Metropolitan Museum of Art, Gift of the Brooklyn Museum, 2009; Gift of Mrs. R. L. Gilpatric, 1960, 2009.300.3781a, b*

149. Tamar Areshidze. "Walking on Water," 2012. Organic glass, nylon threads, leather suede, resin. Courtesy of Tamar Areshidze

150. Prada. Leather Sandal in Mango, Sabbia, and Palissandro Leather, Spring/Summer 2012. Courtesy of Prada USA Corp

151. Rapaport Brothers, Inc. (American). Pair of "Satellite" Jumping Shoes, circa 1955. Metal, textile, rubber. Brooklyn Museum, Gift of Harry Greenberger, 2010.51a, b

152. Damien Hirst (designer). Manolo Blahnik (manufacturer). "Dot" Boots, 2002. Cotton, leather. The Metropolitan Museum of Art, New York, Catharine Breyer Van Bomel Foundation Fund, 2003 (2003.52a, b)

153. Terry de Havilland. Boots, 1979–81. Leather, kid, metal, nylon rubber, synthetic material. The Bata Shoe Museum, P98.0004.AB

154. Conspiracy/Gianluca Tamburini. "Aerial Mardi Gras," 2013. Titanium, leather, glass beads. Courtesy of Conspiracy by Gianluca Tamburini

155. Chanel. "Light Bulb Heel," 2008, "Paris London" Métiers d'Art Collection. Leather, plastic, metal. Courtesy of Chanel

156. threeASFOUR (Gabriel Asfour, Adi Gil, Angela Donhauser). "Mirror Wedge," 2013

157. Rosanne Bergsma. Heel, 2011. Courtesy of Rosanne Bergsma

158. Victoria Spruce. Wedge, 2012. 3-D-printed plastic with sheet napa and leather insole. Courtesy of Victoria Spruce

159. Zuzana Serbak. Heels, 2011. Carbon fiber, goat leather. Courtesy of Zuzana Németh Serbáková

160. threeASFOUR (Gabriel Asfour, Adi Gil, Angela Donhauser). "3-D-Printed Wedge," 2013

161. Nicholas Kirkwood. Wedge, Spring/Summer 2013. Leather. Courtesy of Nicholas Kirkwood

162. Chau Har Lee. Platform, 2010. Perspex. Courtesy of Chau Har Lee

163. Sputniko!. "Healing Fukushima (Nanohana Heels)," 2012. Shoe design by Masaya Kushino. Courtesy of the Artist and SCAI THE BATHHOUSE, Tokyo. Photo © Takuya Shima

164. JANTAMINIAU. "L'Image Tranquille," 2013. (Handcrafted by René van den Berg.) Courtesy of JANTAMINIAU

165. Prada. Wedge Sandal in Rosso, Bianco, and Nero Leather, Spring/Summer 2012. Courtesy of Prada USA Corp.

166. Tamar Areshidze. "Levitating Shoe," 2011. Wood, metal, resin, leather suede, PVC. Courtesy of Tamar Areshidze

167. Giuseppe Zanotti. "Gladiator Boot," Spring/Summer 2013. Courtesy of Giuseppe Zanotti

168. Atalanta Weller. "The Woven Poodle Shoes," 2009. Leather, satin, steel. Courtesy of Atalanta Weller

169. FINSK. "Project 3," 2010. Leather, patent leather, kid suede, hand-painted wood heel. Courtesy of FINSK, by Julia Lundsten

170. Ghada Amer and Reza Farkhondeh. Higher Me (working title), 2014. Film. Courtesy of the artists

171. Zach Gold. 4 Screens, 2014. Wall-mounted video panels, color and black and white, sound. Courtesy of Zach Gold

172. Steven Klein. Untitled, 791, 2014. Film. Courtesy of Steven Klein Studio

173. Nick Knight. La Douleur Exquise, 2014. Film. Courtesy of Nick Knight and SHOWstudio

174. Marilyn Minter. Smash, 2014. Video, color, sound. Courtesy of the artist and Salon 94, New York

175. Rashaad Newsome, Knot, 2014. Single-channel video installation, color, sound. Courtesy of the artist

Works in the Brooklyn presentation
not illustrated in the plates

British. Shoes, 1720–39. Silk, kid.
The Metropolitan Museum of Art,
New York, Purchase, Judith and Gerson
Leiber Fund, 1992 (1992.273a, b)

British. Shoes, 1700–1710. Silk, metal,
leather, wood. The Metropolitan
Museum of Art, New York, Purchase,
Irene Lewisohn and Alice L. Crowley
Bequests, 1984 (1984.141a, b)

Salvatore Ferragamo (Italian,
1898–1960). Sandal, 1937. Leather.
The Metropolitan Museum of Art,
New York, Gift of Salvatore Ferragamo,
1973 (1973.282.3)

Morris Wolock & Co. (American).
Shoe, late 1920s. Leather, lizard,
pearl. The Metropolitan Museum
of Art, New York, Gift of The Guild
of Better Shoe Manufacturers, Inc.,
1948 (C.I.48.12.27)

House of Chanel. Shoes, circa
1996. Silk, leather, metal. The
Metropolitan Museum of Art,
New York, Gift of Thomas L.
Kempner, 2006 (2006.420.134a, b)

Bally of Switzerland. Sandals, circa
1935. Silk, leather. The Metropolitan
Museum of Art, New York, Gift of Ursula
G. Korzenik, 1999 (1999.479a, b)

Manolo Blahnik. "Micamu" Shoes,
Spring/Summer 2006. Silk,
rhinestones. The Metropolitan
Museum of Art, New York, Gift of
Manolo Blahnik, 2006 (2007.46a, b)

Salvatore Ferragamo (Italian,
1898–1960). "Invisible" Sandal, 1947.
Leather. The Metropolitan Museum
of Art, New York, Gift of Salvatore
Ferragamo, 1973 (1973.282.4)

Roger Vivier (French, 1913–1998) for
Agnès b. (French). Shoes, circa 1996.
Leather, elastic, plastic, silk. The
Metropolitan Museum of Art, New York,
Gift of Roger Vivier for Agnès b.,
1999 (1999.475a, b)

Syrian. Sandals, 1920s. Wood, mother-
of-pearl. The Metropolitan Museum
of Art, New York, Gift of Harold Koda,
2002 (2002.164a, b)

Bernard Figueroa (designer).
D'alojo (manufacturer). Mule, circa
1993. Synthetic, leather. Brooklyn
Museum Costume Collection at
The Metropolitan Museum of Art,
Gift of the Brooklyn Museum, 2009;
Gift of Bernard Figueroa, 1996.
2009.300.6113

Saks Fifth Avenue (American). Platform
Sandals, circa 1940. Silk, jute. Brooklyn
Museum Costume Collection at The
Metropolitan Museum of Art, Gift of the
Brooklyn Museum, 2009; Gift of Vivian
Mook Baer in memory of Sylvia Terner
Mook, 1983. 2009.300.5930a, b

**GHADA AMER
AND REZA FARKHONDEH**
Ghada Amer and Reza Farkhondeh, born in Egypt and Iran respectively, collaborate on mixed-media works and videos that have been exhibited at museums and galleries around the world. Their multilayered imagery touches on the confluence of Eastern and Western cultural symbols while exploring female sexuality, pleasure, beauty, identity, and nature. In 2008 the Brooklyn Museum presented a survey of Amer's work, *Ghada Amer: Love Has No End,* which included several of their collaborative drawings.

**GABRIEL ASFOUR, ADI GIL,
AND ANGELA DONHAUSER
(threeASFOUR)**
The designs of the fashion collective threeASFOUR combine a poetic and philosophical mood with high-tech materials and processes such as digital printing, laser cutting, and 3-D printing. A multimedia exhibition of their work, *threeASFOUR: Mer Ka Ba,* was presented at the Jewish Museum in 2013.

BRIAN ATWOOD
After studying at Fashion Institute of Technology and working as a model, Brian Atwood became the first American designer hired by Gianni Versace. He launched his own label in 2001, creating sexy sky-high heels that epitomize glamour.

ZACH GOLD
Photographer and filmmaker Zach Gold is the founder and co-curator of PLAYGROUND, an independent collective that explores and celebrates the experiential relationship between fashion and art. He has exhibited and lectured internationally on fashion and film. His film for the designer A. F. Vandevorst was presented at the Pompidou Center and at the Rotterdam Film Festival, where he was also invited to speak on the subject of fashion films. Gold has shot campaigns and directed videos for many leading companies and fashion houses, including Issey Miyake and Iris van Herpen, and his work is part of the permanent collection of the Metropolitan Museum of Art's Costume Institute.

ZAHA HADID
Zaha Hadid, the founder of Zaha Hadid Architects, is internationally renowned for her innovative and futuristic buildings that integrate landscape

and geology with technology and human-made systems. Hadid was the first woman to receive the Pritzker Architecture Prize, in 2004.

JULIAN HAKES
Julian Hakes is an award-winning architect with a particular interest in engineering and landmark bridge design. After working on many international architectural projects, Hakes created the "Mojito" heel, a unique, 3-D-printed design.

PIERRE HARDY
Pierre Hardy studied dance while completing a degree in fine arts from the École Normale Supérieure in Paris. He worked as a fashion illustrator before designing his first shoe collection in 1988 for Christian Dior. He has designed shoes for Hermès, and in collaboration with Nicolas Ghesquière for Balenciaga, he created some of that label's most progressive shoe designs. Since 1999 he has created his own line of sculptural, architectural shoes.

STEVEN KLEIN
After studying painting at the Rhode Island School of Design, Steven Klein went on to become a photographer and filmmaker recognized for his lush and subversive narrative style and his collaborations with entertainers such as Madonna and Brad Pitt. His fashion editorials and celebrity portraits appear regularly in many international publications, and he has worked on campaigns with designers including Tom Ford, Alexander McQueen, and Dolce & Gabbana.

NICK KNIGHT
Nick Knight is a photographer and filmmaker known for innovative work that challenges conventional ideals of beauty. He is the founder of the fashion website SHOWstudio.com, and his award-winning editorial work has appeared in numerous fashion and other publications. Knight has collaborated on advertising and fashion projects with Christian Dior and Alexander McQueen, among others, and has directed several music videos. The Natural History Museum in London features a permanent installation produced by Knight, and he has displayed his work at the Victoria & Albert Museum and Tate Modern.

REM D. KOOLHAAS (UNITED NUDE)
Architect Rem D. Koolhaas is the creative director and founder of United Nude, launched in 2003 with the signature "Möbius" heel. UN is known for shoes inspired by modern architectural and design concepts, and frequently collaborates on special projects with other designers, such as Iris van Herpen, and architect Zaha Hadid.

MASAYA KUSHINO
Masaya Kushino is a graduate of the Kyoto Institute of Art and Design. After working as a freelance designer and stylist, he started his own label in 2007. His hybrid, animal-inspired high-heel designs have been worn by Lady Gaga.

ALESSANDRA LANVIN (APERLAÏ)
Alessandra Lanvin has degrees in political science and art history and worked for several years in Paris as a luxury-industry recruiter. In 2009 she founded Aperlaï, which has become known for its graphic and architectural high-heel designs.

CHAU HAR LEE
Chau Har Lee creates dynamic and sculptural high-heel designs that bridge traditional shoemaking techniques with new technologies. She holds an MA in footwear design from the Royal College of Art in London and is the recipient of the 2009 ITS Accessories award and the 2009 Manolo Blahnik RCA award.

CHRISTIAN LOUBOUTIN
Christian Louboutin opened his first store in Paris in 1991 and is today acknowledged as one of the primary creative forces in the luxury-shoe market. His sexy, towering designs, all incorporating his signature red sole and frequently embellished with spikes, feathers, and other elegant and exotic materials, have become icons of contemporary high-heel design.

JULIA LUNDSTEN (FINSK)
Julia Lundsten, a graduate of the Royal College of Art in London, is the Finnish shoe designer behind the FINSK label, which was launched in 2004. Her cutting-edge designs are inspired by architecture, furniture, and forms found in nature. In 2007 she won the Finnish Young Designer of the Year award.

MARILYN MINTER
Artist Marilyn Minter's paintings, photographs, and films explore what she calls the "pathology of glamour." Her work has been the subject of numerous solo and group exhibitions around the world. A retrospective of her work is being organized by the Contemporary Art Museum in Houston.

RASHAAD NEWSOME
Rashaad Newsome's mixed-media works in performance, photography, collage, video, sculpture, and sound examine the intersection of heraldry and other traditional arts with the contemporary forms of hip-hop and voguing. His works are widely exhibited, performed, and screened, and in 2013 the New Orleans Museum of Art presented the retrospective exhibition *Rashaad Newsome: King of Arms.*

CAT POTTER
Cat Potter is a footwear designer specializing in conceptual, wearable art. Her experimental shoes mix traditional methods of design and construction with alternative materials and technologies. Potter has an MA in Fashion Footwear from the London College of Fashion.

WINDE RIENSTRA
The architectural designs of Winde Rienstra, a 2009 graduate of the Utrecht School of the Arts, reflect her fascination with structure, geometry, and space. She is particularly known for her towering platform shoes, often created with unconventional and sustainable materials.

ELIZABETH SEMMELHACK
As the Senior Curator of the Bata Shoe Museum, Elizabeth Semmelhack has organized numerous exhibitions exploring the social meaning of footwear, including *Heights of Fashion: A History of the Elevated Shoe; On a Pedestal: From Renaissance Chopines to Baroque Heels;* and *Out of the Box: The Rise of Sneaker Culture.* She has lectured and published extensively on the history of the high heel and has served as a consultant to the Costume Institute at the Metropolitan Museum of Art.

LISA SMALL
Lisa Small, Curator of Exhibitions at the Brooklyn Museum since 2011, was the coordinating curator for the Museum's presentation of *The Fashion World of Jean Paul Gaultier: From the Sidewalk to the Catwalk* and other exhibitions. Prior to joining the Brooklyn Museum, she held curatorial positions at the American Federation of Arts and the Dahesh Museum. She has taught art history at Hunter College, Brooklyn College, and the School of Visual Arts.

Published on the occasion of the
exhibition *Killer Heels: The Art
of the High-Heeled Shoe*, organized
by Lisa Small, Curator of Exhibitions,
Brooklyn Museum.

Exhibition Itinerary
(Venues as of May 15, 2014)
Brooklyn Museum
September 10, 2014–February 15, 2015
Albuquerque Museum
May 30–August 9, 2015

Library of Congress
Cataloging-in-Publication Data:
Killer heels : the art of the high-heeled
shoe / edited by Lisa Small ; essays
by Lisa Small, Stefano Tonchi, and
Caroline Weber; with contributions
by Ghada Amer and Reza Farkhondeh;
Gabriel Asfour, Angela Donhauser,
and Adi Gil; Brian Atwood; Zach
Gold; Zaha Hadid; Julian Hakes; Pierre
Hardy; Steven Klein; Nick Knight;
Rem D. Koolhaas; Masaya Kushino;
Alessandra Lanvin; Chau Har Lee;
Christian Louboutin; Julia Lundsten;
Marilyn Minter; Rashaad Newsome;
Cat Potter; Winde Rienstra; Elizabeth
Semmelhack; and René van den
Berg and Karin Janssen.
pages cm
Includes bibliographical references
and index.
ISBN 978-3-7913-5380-7 --
ISBN 978-0-87273-177-6 (paperback)
1. Shoes--Social aspects.
GT2130.K55 2014
391.4'13--dc23
2014007906

First published in 2014 by
DelMonico Books · Prestel
and Brooklyn Museum

Brooklyn Museum
200 Eastern Parkway
Brooklyn, NY 11238-6052
www.brooklynmuseum.org

in association with DelMonico Books,
an imprint of Prestel Publishing

Prestel, a member of Verlagsgruppe
Random House GmbH

Prestel Verlag
Neumarkter Strasse 28
81673 Munich
Tel.: 49 89 41 36 0
Fax: 49 89 41 36 23 35

Prestel Publishing Ltd.
14–17 Wells Street
London W1T 3PD
Tel.: 44 20 7323 5004
Fax: 44 20 7323 0271

Prestel Publishing
900 Broadway, Suite 603
New York, NY 10003
Tel.: 212 995 2720
Fax: 212 995 2733
E-mail: sales@prestel-usa.com
www.prestel.com

Captions followed by * indicate works
not included in the Brooklyn Museum
presentation.

Full captions for works in the Catalogue
section are included in the Catalogue
Checklist on pages 218–20.

Title page: Roger Vivier. "Virgule
Houndstooth," Fall 2004. Courtesy
of Roger Vivier, Paris (No. 94)

Page 4: Vivienne Westwood. "Super
Elevated Gillies," 1993. Courtesy of
Vivienne Westwood (No. 85)

Page 5: Naomi Campbell, Vivienne
Westwood Autumn/Winter 93/94.
Photo: Niall McInerney. © Bloomsbury
Fashion Photography Archive

Publication of this volume was
organized at the Brooklyn Museum:
James D. Leggio, Head of Publications
and Editorial Services
Project Editor: Joanna Ekman
Picture Research: Alice Cork

For DelMonico Books · Prestel:
Production Manager: Karen Farquhar

Designed by Abbott Miller
with Yoon-Young Chai, Pentagram

Printed in China

PHOTOGRAPHY CREDITS

Plates

Unless otherwise indicated in this
note or in the numbered Catalogue
Checklist captions, all photographs of
contemporary shoes in the Catalogue
section are by Jay Zukerkorn.

All objects from the Brooklyn
Museum Costume Collection at
The Metropolitan Museum of
Art: Brooklyn Museum photograph,
Mellon Costume Documentation
Project, Lea Ingold and Lolly Koon,
photographers. All other numbered
Metropolitan Museum of Art images:
copyright © The Metropolitan
Museum of Art. Image source: Art
Resource, NY

All Metropolitan Museum of Art
thumbnail images in checklist
(except those from the Brooklyn
Museum Costume Collection at
The Metropolitan Museum of Art):
copyright © The Metropolitan
Museum of Art

All Bata Shoe Museum images: © 2014
Bata Shoe Museum, Toronto, Canada.

New photography of Brooklyn Museum
shoes and No. 115 by Sarah DeSantis,
and digitization of selected illustrative
materials by Tracie Davis, Digital
Collections and Services, Brooklyn
Museum

Figures

Unless otherwise specified in the
captions, illustrations are courtesy
of the individuals and institutions
indicated in the captions.